Form and Vision

in

The Novels of Anita Desai

In the same series

Virginia Woolf and Anita Desai
Asha Kanwar

Indian Women Novelists (18 vols)
R.K. Dhawan, ed.

Feminism and Recent Fiction in English
Sushila Singh, ed.

Nayantara Sahgal and Doris Lessing
Neena Arora

Kamala Markandaya and Ruth Jhabvala
Rekha Jha

Form and Vision
in
The Novels of Anita Desai

Sandhyarani Dash

PRESTIGE

Published by
Prestige Books
New Delhi 110 008

1996

Reprint 1999

Photo Typesetting by
Pivot Computers
Delhi 110 006
Ph. 2934490

Printed at
Mehra Offset Press
New Delhi 110 002

Contents

Preface

The book presents a synoptic view of Anita Desai's fiction in terms of her major themes and techniques. It aims at evaluating her novels in view of the shifting sensibilities and changing attitudes as India moves from a conservative and traditional social order to a liberal and open socio-cultural ethos. As an artist Desai's concern is with the predicament of the individual vis-a-vis the social forces that try to subvert human identity. The book examines the narrative mode of Desai in the context of the socio-psychological implications of the novels. It is suggested that Anita Desai's emphasis on the study of the individual as an aggregate of psychic and emotional impulses leads her to write what might be called novels of character. City, nature and childhood memory play important roles in the shaping of Desai's form and vision. The urban milieu provides an artistic backdrop to her novels and the city assumes a symbolic dimension that reflects the existential anguish of the tormented souls who are in constant quest of self-hood. It is suggested that the city not only reveals a realistic view of life but also becomes the very metaphor of existence. Nature is presented in the novels as a metaphor of hope and life and as an ironic presence that sharpens the awareness of a grim reality. Nature provides a symbolic dimension to the total meaning of Desai's fiction and thus becomes a shaping element of her form and style. The memories of childhood help the characters to understand and evaluate their present. Thus the rites of childhood become an effective strategy that sharpens a tragic sense of life which pervades the fictional world of Desai.

Anita Desai's vision of life is one of ambivalence which encompasses defeat and disillusionment as well as acceptance and affirmation. Desai's ultimate vision is controlled by a profound sense of the tragic.

Though there are a large number of critiques of Desai's fiction, this book can claim an originality of approach in terms of the fresh organization of various perceptions and interpretations. I shall feel amply rewarded if the book is well received by students and research scholars.

The book is dedicated to the memory of my father and mother whose inspiration guided me to venture on this project and complete it.

Words may fail to express my deep gratitude to Dr. J.N. Patnaik, Director, Institute of English Language Teaching, Orissa, Bhubaneswar, for his inspiring guidance at every step.

I am immensely grateful to Dr. Mohit Ray, Professor and Head of the Department of English, Burdwan University, for his valuable counsels. I am very much thankful to my husband Dr. S.B. Parida, Lecturer in Pol. Sc., V.N. College, without whose co-operation the work would not have been completed. Also, I must thank my son Ashirvad and daughter Amrita for patiently bearing with me all through the strenuous years of the preparation of this manuscript.

I am extremely thankful to Ms. D. Renu, Director, Prestige Books, New Delhi, for bringing out the book expeditiously and so elegantly.

SANDHYARANI DASH

The Narrative Mode: Form and Meaning

The debate on the legitimacy of Indian writing in English that had once preoccupied the academics and intellectuals of India has now been resolved. That Indian English writing can embody genuine Indian experience is no more questioned today. On the other hand the proliferation of critical responses both in India and abroad towards Indian writing in English shows that despite the problems of writing in a second language, the Indian writers in English have been able to articulate the typical Indian milieu and experience with skill and authenticity. It therefore does not seem anymore necessary to defend a novelist like Anita Desai against the charges of untenability of English writing in India. The fact that Anita Desai has achieved great distinction as a novelist and has drawn a great deal of critical attention is enough to assert that she is among the foremost Indian English writers of fiction.

Much of the critical writing on Anita Desai centres round her preoccupation with the urban sensibility and a style of what she herself calls the "language of the interior." When Meena Belliappa had asserted as far back as in 1971 that Anita Desai's novels marked "a departure from current modes of fiction writing," (1) she obviously had in mind Anita Desai's distinctive qualities that were unlike those of the stalwarts of an earlier generation particularly of R.K. Narayan, Mulk Raj Anand, Raja Rao and Bhabani Bhattacharya. The shift in sensibility from this earlier generation of writers to Anita Desai and for that matter Kamala Markandaya and Ruth Prawer Jhabvala is indicative of the socio-cultural changes India has undergone from the forties to the sixties and seventies. While the major preoccupation of Narayan, Rao, Anand and Bhattacharya is sociological, in terms of hunger, poverty, superstition and dogma, the new generation of Indian English novelists such as Anita Desai and Markandaya is basically concerned with deep cultural and philosophical problems that inevitably emerge in a transitional society. The present study on the form and vision of Anita Desai aims at evaluating her novels in terms of the shifting sensibilities and changing attitudes as India moves from a conservative and traditional social order to a liberal and open socio-cultural ethos. This is not to say that Anita Desai's novels are mere sociological documents or mirrors of Indian reality. She is basically an artist responding to the fundamental questions of human existence and identity. Desai's concern is with the predicament of the individual vis-a-vis the social forces that try to subvert human identity. Anita Desai's emphasis on the study of the individual as an aggregate of the psychic and emotional impulses leads to what might be called the novels of character.

Desai sees her novels as a "pattern or a design," that imposes itself on her imagination: "shutting out all other conflicting patterns that might be there, I begin to put in the pieces." (*Questionnaire,* 5) These pieces are "snatches of conversation, faces glimpsed, insomniac thoughts, reactions to one's reading—an accumulation of sensation and experience dredged up from the depth of one's memory." (5) She prefers the word "pattern" to plot or plan, and considers her method as what Hopkins termed as "inscape." Her novels do not have themes perceived in terms of the linear progression of a story. On the other hand, while writing a novel she "relies on flashes of vision." (5) Desai confesses that characters rather than the story are her central concern: "Story, action and drama mean little to me except in so far as they emanate directly from the characters I am writing about, born of their dreams, wills and actions." (4) Thus the form of her novels is governed by the people who inhabit her fictional world. Their words, deeds, creeds and manners together form a pattern of complex relationships and actions. The plots of the novels seek a form that contains all the ambiguities, complexities and contradictions inherent in the inevitable interactions among characters as well as in their own thoughts and actions.

Desai's protagonists are basically tragic characters. They fail to cope with their surroundings and are cut off from their families and society. They are psychologically disturbed, morbid, self-absorbed and incoherent in their manners and expression. They do not have the determination and the steadiness of will to pursue a definite line of action. They are introverts, "people temporarily fallen into a state of abnormal passiveness to sensation, in which again the association of ideas is not directed and controlled by a "sense for conduct." (Beach, 518) Desai justifies her selection of solitary and introspective characters in the following words: "Well, I think, solitary and introspective people are always very aware of living on the brink. I suppose, every one of us is in a sense aware of living on the brink. Anyone of us might one day face an experience which may push one over, but perhaps my introspective characters are more aware than others are of what lies on the other side." ("Interview," *Stairs to the Attic,* 10)

Her characters are creatures of habit, stubborn and unyielding.

They do not want to lead "the lives of what Sartre would call *Mauvais foi,* bad faith." (Rao, 1982:75) Some of them are defeated but most of them "succeed in saying 'no' to society." (75) These characters are inevitably confronted with an unfriendly and hostile reality. They feel emotionally estranged from the family and environment. They turn inward and speak to themselves in long soliloquies and monologues. Desai adopts the "stream of consciousness" technique in the limited sense of what Arnold Kettle calls "a mode of recollection." (127) Maya, Monisa, Tara, Bim and Nirode—all live on recollections of things past. The context of subjective introspection which holds the key to the meaning of Anita Desai's fiction finds its appropriate medium in the "language of the interior": "Even when two characters meet, they use this particular type of language . . . the language of their thoughts, their interior selves which has nothing to do with geography and can be written in any language." (Desai, *Language Forum,* 225)

The language of the interior serves her purpose best when she dramatizes the innermost feelings of a character in a long soliloquy:

> It became more and more difficult to continue my restless pursuit of window after window. The heat expanded, the bubble shrank. The pressure was tremendous, suffocating. My feet dragged and my body pushed against the resistant atmosphere, as though I were wading. Wading out of my depth. It was all strange, deathly, strange. Innocence turning to guilt. Lilac to purple. Ochre to ugliness. Step by step. All silently. (*Cry, the Peacock,* 184)

With this soliloquy of Maya "we enter an entirely private and introspective territory," (Mukherjee, 1970:27-33) where Maya, a psychologically disturbed woman, obsessed with the idea of death is driven to a schizophrenic state like Sarala in Shakuntala Srinagesh's *The Little Blackbox.* Faulkner also uses this method in *The Sound and Fury* to portray the character of the imbecile who like Maya suffers from a suicidal mania.

Monisha also, like Maya, soliloquizes about her meaningless and uninvolved existence:

> To pretend to have forgotten, to pretend to believe in these trivialities, these pettinesses of our mean existence—is that right? . . .
>
> The family here, and their surroundings tell me such a life cannot be lived—a life dedicated to nothing—that this husk is a protection from death. Ah yes, yes, then it is a choice between

> death and mean existence, and that, surely, not a difficult choice. (*Voices in the City*, 121-22)

The actions of the protagonists determine the plot or theme of Desai's novels. It is a quality of the dramatic novel to show that "both appearance and reality are the same, and that character is action and action character." (Muir, 47) Desai is interested in "delving deeper and deeper into a character or scene rather than going round about it." (Jain, 14)

Desai follows the triptyche structure in four of her novels: *Cry, the Peacock, Bye-Bye, Blackbird, Where Shall We Go This Summer?* and *Fire on the Mountain*. Part I and Part III of the novel *Cry, the Peacock* are very brief consisting of three and eleven pages respectively. Part I works like a prologue to the novel which describes the conditions which lead Maya to her neurosis. Maya is a childless woman who thinks that the death of her pet dog Toto is a sure prelude to another great and impending tragedy. Her preoccupation with death had been actually planted long ago in her childhood by the albino astrologer's prophecy foretelling the death of either of the couple after her marriage. The other causes of her suffering are her marriage to Gautama, a man of her father's age who is detached and reserved even to the extent of not fulfilling her physical and emotional needs. The indifferent behaviour of Gautama's family members increases her sense of loneliness which gradually develops into an actual sense of alienation. In part III Maya regresses back to an infantile state and finally leaps to death.

Bye-Bye, Blackbird begins with Dev's arrival in London and his frustration in a foreign country. In Part II, "Discovery and Recognition," Dev develops a fascination for London. In Part III Adit feels homesick and his attitude towards London undergoes a change. Thematically the novel is similar to Kamala Markandaya's *The Nowhere Man,* Timeri Murari's *The Marriage* and V.S. Naipaul's *The Mimic Men.* Structurally it follows the pattern of Anatole France's *Thais.* Thais is a courtesan and leads a sinful life in Alexandria whereas Paphnuce is a good man who lives in the desert. When the two characters meet, they change their places. After the meeting with Paphnuce, Thais goes to a monastery and gets salvation because she met Paphnuce, a good person. But Paphnuce is damned as he met Thais. Just as the characters change in inverse proportion in Anatole France's novel, similarly the two characters Dev and Adit converge and cross in Desai's *Bye-Bye, Blackbird.* In the beginning there is an anglophobia in Dev whereas Adit has a deep rooted liking for England. But in Part II the characters change their places. Dev's anglophobia changes to anglophilia and Adit's anglophilia changes to anglophobia. There is also a different type of discovery for Adit. He realizes that his appreciation and weakness for England is only a pretence and he must go back to India to let his son take birth in his homeland. The last part, "Departure," describes the return of the blackbird to its permanent nest which provides unity to the novel. R.S. Sharma calls this novel a dramatic poem, as it employs the metaphor of voyage or quest to suggest "a pattern of action where each soul, after initial shock, puzzlement and anguish, discovers Its own natural condition. The trisection plan of the novel, 'Arrival,' 'Discovery' and 'Recognition and Departure,' also seems to suggest this pattern." (*Literary Criterion,* 48) He further says that "too much authorial intrusion is resorted to achieve this end." (48)

In *Where Shall We Go This Summer?* Part I, "Monsoon 67," starts in the present and deals with Sita's abnormal thoughts of escaping the process of creation. It is followed by "Winter 47" which depicts the reminiscences of her childhood in Manori. Part III "Monsoon 57" comes back to the present. Sita moves through three stages, thesis, antithesis and synthesis or doubt, rejection and acceptance. Vimala Rao, comparing the structure of this novel with Virginia Woolf's *To the Lighthouse* says: "The action of the first section takes place on the island of Manori, in the present time of Sita's life, that of the second in her past, and the third in what she has accepted as her future. The manipulation of time and space to depict the extraordinary inner consciousness of Sita is especially reminiscent of Woolf in *To the Lighthouse*." (46)

Desai follows a triptyche structure also in *Fire on the Mountain.* Part I of the novel, "Nanda Kaul at Carignano," describes Nanda Kaul's life of a 'recluse' in Carignano where she does not want anybody to interrupt her privacy. In Part II, "Raka Comes to Carignano," Desai depicts Raka's arrival and its impact on Nanda while Part III "Ila Das Leaves Carignano" depicts the violent rape and murder of Ila Das and the breakdown of Nanda Kaul's make-believe world. As Shanta Acharya observes, in *Fire on the Mountain*, "stylistically there is greater sensitivity and restraint in the portrayal of theme that is common to all four of her novels." (1-4) Comparing the structure of *Fire on the Mountain* with a film scenario, Madhusudan Prasad says: "This novel has obviously been written on the pattern of a film scenario as all its chapters are strikingly short focussing only on particular scenes or episodes with marvellous vividity and verbal economy expected only of a rare genius." (102) The story begins in the tranquil and serene hills of Carignano. The movement is very slow but the end is violently climactic. With her great power of lyricism, evocative imagery and symbols, Desai "knits together various stairs of the story in one unit." (Atma Ram, *Triveni*)

Voices in the City and *Clear Light of Day* are divided into four parts. In *Voices in the City*, the four parts are entitled "Nirode," "Monisha," "Amla" and "Mother," each part devoted to a leading character of the novel. In *Clear Light of Day* Desai treats the existential theme of Time and its influence on human beings. Part I of the book is a record of things past and present. While Part II celebrates the memories of the past, Part III describes the childhood of the major characters. As in other novels, in this novel also Desai adopts the flashback technique to describe the childhood of Tara, Bim, Raja and Baba. The narrative shifts from the past to the present, almost in the jigsaw fashion. Though she portrays a series of incidents, Desai abandons the role of the chronicler and tries her best to weave a refreshing pattern of reality. *In Custody*, unlike other novels of Desai, is divided into eleven chapters. The action of the novel has a pendular motion as it shifts back and forth between Mirpore and Delhi.

The narrative in Part I and III of *Cry, the Peacock* is in third person whereas in Part II of the novel it is in the first person. In the final section the writer turns omniscient, with a final authorial comment at the end of the novel: "They met for an instance, there was silence, and then both disappeared into the dark quiet. All around the dark was quiet then." (218)

The entire novel, *Voices in the City*, except Part III is presented in third person narrative. Part III of the novel is in the first person in terms of Monisha's diary. In *Fire on the Mountain,* through an "adroit manipulation of point of view" (Sharma, *Littcrit,* 6) Desai shows her control over her fictive world. Though most of her novels are in third person, the novelist nevertheless stands apart and allows the characters maximum freedom to grow as a good writer does. In the words of Percy Lubbock: "This is not 'my' story, says the author, you know nothing of me; it is the story of this man or woman in whose words you have it, and he or she is a person whom you 'can' know; and you may see for yourselves how the matter arose, the man and woman being such as they are, it all hangs together, and it makes a solid and significant piece of life." (147)

In Desai's novels characters are set in binary opposition in terms of values, attitudes, temperaments and outlook on life. These characters are contrasted in terms of human relationships as between Maya and Gautama, Monisha and Jiban, Sita and Raman. The male characters are also contrasted with each other as between Deven and Murad, Nirode and Dharma, Arun and Nirode. The characters are polarised in terms of social status, success and quality of life. Like the men, the women characters are also polarised. Amla and Monisha are different in their attitudes. When Monisha accepts her defeat and commits suicide being afraid of the stupendous burden of existence, Amla continues by accepting the challenges bravely. Similarly Tara and Bim are also opposed to each other. Tara has a regressive tendency. She likes to go back to her past and gets pleasure in remembering her childhood but Bim is fed up with her childhood and she does not like to be reminded of such a childhood. The character of Sarah in *Bye-Bye, Blackbird* is perhaps the strongest woman character in Desai's fiction who faces the challenges of reality and through silent suffering proves herself as the boldest of all characters in Desai's novels, whereas Desai's other heroines like Maya, Monisha, Sita and Nanda Kaul are afraid of reality and fail to adjust themselves to their present conditions. In *Fire on the Mountain*, the characters of Nanda and Raka are also set in binary opposition. If Nanda is a "recluse out of vengeance" for a life of duties and responsibilities, Raka is a child of loneliness. From the tension between the two emerges the theme of the novel.

The use of fantasy is another important narrative method in Desai. It is by the use of the "disexpected" (Rabkin, 1325) rather than the unexpected that she creates an uncanny atmosphere in her novels. These novels with an element of fantasy in them have "an improvised air, which is the secret of their force and charm." (Forster, 109) Desai uses fantasy in her novels as a narrative technique and also to reinterpret reality. Fantasy becomes a part of the total structure of her novels and it is constantly projected along with and in contrast to the world of reality.

In *Cry, the Peacock* the protagonist Maya clings to fantasy because she is unable to cling to reality. Her relationship to reality passes through three different stages, her childhood, marital life and finally when she totally surrenders herself to the world of insanity. The conflict between the two worlds of fantasy and reality is perceived when at the beginning of the novel, after the death of the dog, Maya rushes to the garden tap "to wash the vision from her eyes." To make herself free from the burden of the present Maya recedes to her past. She remembers her father's garden, the breakfast in the morning which was like a revel of fairies and elves, the fairy stories of the "Arabian Nights," tales from Indian mythology, "tales of princes and regal queens of jackals and tigers" which have an element of fantasy in them. Maya lives in a state of fear and with hallucinations. Fear is only a projection of her mind as it is baseless and abnormal. She senses the cruel trainer behind the bear dance seen in her childhood and has nightmarish experiences during night. The image of the Kathakali dancer comes to her as a "phantom gone berserk." She considers Gautama as an "unreal ghost," a "body without a heart." There are several uncanny references like this throughout the novel. Thus there is a constant interaction between illusion and reality in Anita Desai's fictional world.

In *Where Shall We Go This Summer?* fantasy is used to reinterpret reality. The magic island of Manori, Sita's father who is a protective figure in the island like Prospero, her desire to keep the child unborn and several other references have an element of fantasy in them.

In *Fire on the Mountain*, Nanda Kaul, Ram Lal and Raka have all their own worlds of fantasy woven into their perception of reality. Raka's world of "male and female monsters" is juxtaposed with the morbid world of her parents:

> as she ran, her sweating fists beating her sides and her feet tearing through thorns, ferns and gravel. All the caged, clawed, tailed, headless male and female monster followed her, pell-mell, prancing to the tune of the Bridge on the river Kwai. "Ta-ra-ta-ra ta-ra. Somewhere behind them, behind it all, was her father home from a party, stumbling and crashing through the curtains of night, his mouth opening to let out a flood of rotten stench, beating at her mother with hammers and fists and abuse. (71)

Nanda Kaul creates a fantastic world by telling imaginary stories to Raka about her childhood. Her projected childhood is an attempt to create the bond of love between herself and Raka. She also derives a sort of childhood pleasure of which she herself was deprived in her childhood. Nanda Kaul thinks, "fantasy and fairytale had their place in life." (89) In the storm abated evening when Nanda and Raka are sitting in the drawing room, Raka touches the little bronze Buddha which leads Nanda to weave a fantastic story. She suddenly begins in a "high, musical voice that did not sound as if it belonged to her." (82) Nanda tells Raka, "it comes all the way from Tibet, you know. My father bought it." (82) Though Raka is a "selective" listener, she patiently listens to Nanda: "That was long, long ago at a time—Nanda begins her story." (82) She describes her father as one who "wore leather boots up to his knees as he rode away, and the two flaps of his fur caps showed like ears, for a long way. His dog, a black Bhotiya we called Demon followed him. They all splashed through the icy river and disappeared on the rocks." (83)

Raka listens to Nanda at the beginning but gradually she is bored and becomes suspicious and wants to be released from this disagreeable intimacy. She is "stifled inside the old lady's words, dreams and more words. She yawned with boredom." (100) Raka's world of fantasy is shaped by her memory of the past. She thinks of the factory as a "square dragon." Ram Lal tells her about the fancy dress ball where ladies are dressed like queens and men like princes. But inside the club Raka finds "madmen and rioters" (69) who appear like monsters chasing each other. But behind this world of fear lies another world in her subconscious: the world of her childhood.

Fantasy, juxtaposed with reality, brings out a change of perspective in the realization of reality in Desai's novels. It becomes a part of the narrative and makes clear the difference between the illusive world of the protagonists and the reality outside.

Anita Desai's narrative mode frequently soars into poetic heights in tune with the intensity of perception embodied in the novels:

> Had it come? I ran to the window, the balls of my feet turned to truckles. No this was a beginning and not an end. Storm. Motion. Speed. Living I beat upon the window as the dancer, waiting to go on stage, pounds the earth with uncontrollable feet once the hypnotic drumming begins. What agony in ecstasy, what pain in magnificence. (*Cry, the Peacock*, 188)

Her minute observation of reality is reflected in her rich prose style:

> A soft November mist rose from the river, like stream from a cauldron, but cool, frozen stream, the tide was out, the water low and a slow motion rocked the big ships, brazenly illuminated by giant lamps as cranes worked overtime at loading and unloading coal, jute, swaths of pink and white cotton, a tiger in a cage—in a kind of subdued uproar. (*Voices in the City*, 9)

The narrative mode of Anita Desai's fiction is controlled by the characters, who in their freedom to act and think weave a pattern of existence and a form of meaning through the various strategies of triptyche structure, first person and third person narrative, fantasy and poetic intensity.

The Anguish of Exile: City and Sensibility

The city has been the focus of all modern literature and much of the sensibility that has gone into the creation of great literary works, such as T.S. Eliot's *Waste Land* and James Joyce's *Ulysses* which have been shaped by an acute awareness of the decadence of human values in the mechanistic ethos of the modern metropolis.

Anita Desai's perception of Indian life basically centres round the apparent glitter and essential squalor of the modern city. While R.K. Narayan, Mulk Raj Anand and Bhabani Bhattacharya look at Indian life from the perspective of its traditions and values that are rooted essentially in villages and the villagefolk, Anita Desai, like her contemporaries Kamala Markandaya, Arun Joshi, Ruth Prawer Jhabvala and Nayantara Sahgal, comprehends life in its essential rootlessness fostered by the growth of the metropolis that inhibits human essence in the welter of utilitarianism and materialism.

Desai's novels not only embody a realistic view of the city with its "sick hurry and divided aims," but also encompass it as a metaphor of existence that sharpens the ironic mode of her fiction. The city eventually assumes a symbolic dimension that reflects existential anguish of the tormented souls who are in constant quest of selfhood. The urban milieu provides an artistic backdrop to her novels and the city becomes an overbearing 'presence.' The characters are stifled by the constant pressure of the urban milieu which not only induces a sense of vacuum and chaos but also intensifies the sense of despair and alienation in the individual.

The city in *Cry, the Peacock* is best perceived by the minor characters, such as Mrs. Lal, the prim lady at the party, the Sikh, the cabaret dancers, Gautama's mother and sister Nila. The protagonist Maya stands as a victim of the constant tension between the vain-glory of city life and her regressive tendency to recapture the childhood world of innocence and purity. The city of Delhi acts in this novel as a compulsive presence which, with the parties, dances, drinks and gossips in the club, disturbs the inner quiet of the protagonist.

The party at Mrs. Lal's house is a symbolic revelation of the attitudes, temperaments and life-styles of the people who live in the metropolis. It is a gathering of strangers who apparently have no "aggressive or defensive weapons" against each other, though, in reality, these weapons are there, hidden and suppressed. The objective of the party is no more than mere collection of information about the neighbours, an attempt to probe into the "muddy depths of our neighbour's minds," and at the same time a hypocritical attempt at "social graces into the bargain." The two ladies at the party, Mrs. Lal and the prim lady, are the symbolic representatives of the sham of the metropolis. Their conversation reveals the different facets of life in the urban milieu. There is theft in the neighbourhood, gossip in the clubs, and parties at the park.

As the party continues, Mrs. Lal's small son trails into the room. The mother is so busy and indifferent that she barely notices the child and absently tells him to go and play, even though the time is past ten o'clock. The child's appearance leads Maya to reflect on the indifference which would slowly kill the youngest, freshest generation and they have no hope of survival. (70)

Mrs. Lal feels very awkward and nervous at the prim lady's question: "Have you no ayah?" Looking at the four sleeping daughters inside a patched mosquito net, sweating profusely, she again asks, "you have no air conditioner?" in a tone that is "amused and hateful." Mrs. Lal gets so embarrassed that she drifts away to her "pot-bellied husband," knocking the plate of rice and pickles and hitting her forehead against his chin. The Sikh takes it as a joke and calls it an "accident." The word "accident" is picked up by Mrs. Lal to explain "the accidental part" of what Maya sees from the swell of her stained limp clothes, that "she was pregnant." (72)

Maya recollects the cabaret dance, the "ghastly, ghastly cabaret" with such abomination that she says, "I wish we had not let the Singhs take us out after dinner." (73) The "rainbow light" around the bandstand, the Goan drummer, the dancer girls who are of even height with "flopping loose hair" and "muscled legs" and bare bodies arouse chuckles of delight and excitement in the audience. The bouncing movements and acrobatic feats of the girls that shamelessly display their bosoms fills Maya with disdain. The cabaret reveals in its banal glow "a seething mass of pimps and lechers, of touts and prostitutes" (86) who wear the mask of civilization.

Arjuna, Maya's only brother finds the city and his father's world of drinks at the club, parties on the lawn, badminton, flower and poetry to be meaningless. He joins the Quit India movement and disappears. After a long interval of time, he sends a letter to Maya from New York where he works in a canning factory. In spite of his aversion to city life, Arjuna helplessly clings to it. He becomes a victim of the oppressive currents of the city. He is not paid much in the factory. Sometimes it becomes very difficult for him to make both ends meet. But he does not bother as life itself to Arjuna is meaningless, "no matter how elegantly lived." (137) There are also references to the life-style of the poor in Delhi in *Cry, the Peacock*. Maya recollects a past incident of Arjuna being scolded by his father for staying at the house of a friend, a Dhobi's son. The Mohammeds live in a "disreputable" area of the city where "tailor-shops jostled the butchers and people slept out on the street on string beds at night." (134)

The members of Gautama's family, his mother and sister Nila, are like the city itself, callous and indifferent to human relationships. Nila is an unhappily married woman who tries to divorce her husband, whereas Maya feels imprisoned in her in-laws's house. Gautama's mother praises the taste and life-style of her daughter who keeps "artist's hours" by sleeping all through the day and playing Sitar at night. She feels that Nila needs "human company of young, gay people with plenty of ideas and ambitions and occupations." (158) Nila and her mother spend money on fun and frivolity which is displayed when they visit the Connaught Circus. They buy different things, sarees, slippers, balloons till they spend all the money and no money is left to pay the taxi driver. Gautama's mother suggests to take a town bus because it would be less expensive.

The characters have contrasted response to the city life. Arjuna quits the city and joins the freedom movement but again lives in a city like New York under circumstantial compulsion. The Sikh, Mrs. Lal, Nila and her mother—all reflect a positive attitude to the life in the metropolis. They like it and cling to its glitter and pretensions. Gautama on the other hand is the detached and reserved lawyer who like the Buddha believes that attachment to any thing leads to suffering. But the city with its agents, such as the cabaret, the parties, drinks and its fashionable people maddens the protagonist Maya. The death-wish in her deepens which comes "whispering over vast distances," and leads her to declare: "I have to go . . . I must go." (86)

City plays a crucial role in widening the marital gap between Gautama and Maya. Gautama is the busy lawyer who does not want to be "interrupted in his thinking" by such trivial matters as the death of a pet dog. When Maya tells him about the death of Toto, he accepts it as a natural happening. But for Maya, it is the prelude to some great disaster about to happen. She feels estranged from Gautama's world. Even if she wishes to enter it, Gautama never allows her: "On his part, understanding was scant, love was meagre." (90) She feels the absence of Gautama in the house for long hours and whenever he comes, he gets busy with his clients or discusses about politics or philosophy which do not interest Maya. She feels rejected, and utterly lonely in the house: "His coldness, his coldness and incessant talk of cups of tea and philosophy in order not to hear me talk, and talking reveal myself. It is that—My loneliness in this house." (9)

Maya's marriage with Gautama is fixed by her father because Gautama is a close friend of his. Their relationship is neither true nor abiding. It is repeatedly broken and put together again like "sacred icons" which, because of the pettiest superstition they cannot "bear to part." (40) Her loneliness in the house is paradoxically the result of her too much of attachment. It is not for the lack of love for Gautama that she suffers, but for too much of love for him. Maya's feeling of alienation emerges basically from her total disillusionment with the life of the metropolis that has scant regard for abiding emotional relationships. Maya feels exasperated at Gautama's cold response to her physical and emotional needs: "there were countless nights when I had been tortured by a humiliating sense of neglect, of loneliness, of desperation that would not have existed had I not loved him so, had he not meant so much." (201)

Maya's perception of the world around her is in terms of the warmth and profundity of relationships that transcends the insipid and commercial relationships of which Gautama is the symbol. Her disillusionment with the life in her in-laws's family leads her to seek solace from the non-human world of Nature that reflects a sense of harmony in contrast to the discordant quality of urban life. Nature comforts her as well as heightens her loneliness. The lonely stars, isolated from others deepens her sense of isolation when she looks at the night's sky. The "darkness" speaks of distance, separation and loneliness. It breeds frustration, nostalgia and obsession with the past. Maya's alienation from the family as well as from the society is suggested through the images of the train, the caged monkey and the death-cry of the peacock. The images of the death cry of the peacock and the dance of Shiva offer a way out of her existing state. The peacocks dance when they see the rain. They fight before they mate. Their dance like the dance of Shiva is a dance of liberation. It is also a dance of death because they know that they and their lovers are all to die. Still then they are happy: "Living they are aware of Death. Dying, they are in love with life." (110) Maya is also preoccupied with the morbid fear of death. In a state of utter loneliness she remarks, "Torture, guilt, dread, imprisonment—these were the four walls of my private hell, one that no one could survive in long. Death was certain." (110)

This obsession drives Maya to a state of insanity. She herself confesses: "Yes, I am going insane. I am moving further and further from all wisdom, all calm, and I shall soon be mad, if I am not that already." (32) In this state of frenziedness she thinks: "It was now to be either Gautama or I." And finally she opts for Gautama who, if killed, "will not miss life, as he is admittedly 'detached' and indifferent to life." (M. Prasad, 13)

Maya experiences a dust storm outside which corresponds to a similar storm inside her, shaking her up completely. She leads Gautama to the roof and pushes him down to death. He passes through "an immensity of air, down to the very bottom." (208)

Three days after this incident Gautama's mother and sister take her to her father's house in Lucknow and it is understood that she would be admitted into an asylum. But during the night the two women hear a cry of horror and rush upstairs and find "the bright frantic one on the balcony screaming. They met for an instant, there was silence, and then both disappeared into the dark quiet." (218)

Desai depicts the disgusting ugliness and sordidness of the city of Calcutta and the existential anguish of the characters who inhabit it in the novel *Voices in the City*. Nirode's mother and her three children come to Calcutta and are lost in the city of Goddess Kali. They are lost in the "coagulated blaze of light," in the sound and odour of Calcutta which seeks to "absorb outsiders into its culturai foliage." (Singh, 171) Monisha is disturbed by the violence, murder and crime in the city. She is tired of its crowd. It is a deceptively quiet crowd, "passive but distressed till there is a reason for anger and then a sullen yellow flame of bitterness and sarcasm starts up, and it is vicious, mordant." (118) The anger that affects the people of this metropolis is like a "pus-filled boil" that "broods and festers." There is chaos everywhere in the city which corresponds to the disordered and chaotic life that the protagonists live. During examinations, students overturn their desks, destroy the question papers and go on strike. They burn the trams and destroy public properties.

The city has no conscience. Her uncle takes Monisha for sightseeing and she sees the Belur Math, the Jain temple, the Kali temple and the New Market. Besides, she has an encounter with the real life of the city. She sees "vast businessmen" sitting, picking their teeth and "speculatively waggling their feet." Here dwell the greedy people, the cut-throats. Monisha finds no ethics in these houses of trade, "ethics are shunned, all is shunned except the swelling and fattening of the iron safe and of mortal, male flesh." (117) She finds the city a "dull vacant and hopeless face." The streets are full of rickshaw, coolie, the street sweeper, the tanner, the beggar child with his limbs cut off at the joint and the refugees.

Outside the house there is crowd, disturbances and violence and inside the four walls of the house, she feels "locked in a steel container," "a thick glass cubicle," in which she lives without any "touch of love or warmth" from her in-laws. She says: "I am locked apart from all of them, they cannot touch me." (240) In her in-laws's house Monisha is treated like a non-entity. Like Maya, she is also childless and therefore subject to severe criticism: "Like a burst of wild feathers released full in my face, comes the realization that they are talking of me, my organs, the reasons I cannot have a child." (117) She does all the domestic chores like cutting the vegetables, serving food and brushing the children's hair. In the house, crowded with aunts, uncles and relatives, Monisha longs for privacy: "only I wish I were given some tasks I could do alone, in privacy, away from the aunts and uncles, the cousins and nieces and nephews. Alone, I could work better, and I should feel more-whole." (113)

Monisha's marital life is a re-enactment of the Maya-Gautama relationship. Like Maya, she is also frustrated, lonely and alienated. Her longing for touch and intimacy, her lack of communication with her husband make her existence dull and insignificant. She broods on the futility of her existence. Her life enclosed in a steel container is a mere waste. She spends the life of an observer, a handicapped observer and in utter dejection, she cries out, "I have not given birth, I have not attended death. All the intervening drama has gone by, unwound itself like a silent, blurred film that has neither entertained nor horrified me." (115) Her relationship with her husband Jiban is marked "only by loneliness." She has been degraded to the level of a thief being alleged of stealing money from her husband's pocket without his knowledge. Instead of asserting his wife's right to do so, Jiban supports his mother: "He did not say, why did you not tell them at once? He said, why did not you tell me before you took it?" (240)

Being accused of theft by people who themselves are "so low," she thinks "it is to be laid on a level lower than the common earth." The only escape from this state of existence is to accept solitude and to be in exile: "I find on this level that solitude that becomes me most naturally. I am willing to accept this status then, and to live there, a little beyond and below everyone else, in exile." (138)

The world of her in-laws is different from hers. They have "indoor minds, starless and dark-less," but hers is "all darkness now, the blessing it is." (156) She thinks about the Bengali women who work for centuries inside the "barred windows." They await death as they do everything: "The eyes of these silent Bengali women are not dead, but they anticipate death, as they do everything, with resignation." (121) Monisha frantically tries to search for a real meaning in her life, but feels utterly frustrated: "To pretend to have forgotten, to pretend to believe in these trivialities, these pettinesses of our mean existence." (121) She finds no alternative to her confused despair, "the family here, and their surroundings, tell me such a life cannot be lived—a life dedicated to nothing." (122) She has to make a choice between death and mean existence and she thinks probably it is not a very difficult choice.

In the great metropolis, Calcutta, the city of Goddess Kali, Monisha searches for silence. The city has so shaped the minds of its inhabitants that they, like Jiban's family members, have become indifferent to all human feelings, sympathy and love. Monisha discovers two faces of Calcutta, "one rapacious one weary." The city of Goddess Kali is a city of death for her: "Do you hear me, city of Calcutta? City of Kali, Goddess of Death. Not one word from you, I said, not a sound. No shriek, no groan, no cry. I come here for silence, my few moments of night silence, so cease your moaning and wailing awhile." (138) In the process of her existential search she ultimately discovers that it is the absence of love, of "elemental love" that has made her and her brother Nirode "such abject rebels, such craven tragedians." (135)

This absence of love is apparent in her relationship with Jiban, which is "filled only by loneliness and a desperate urge to succeed," and her relationship with her mother, "filled with an in-bred and invalid sense of duty, of honour, of concern." (135-36) Monisha's mental agony increases and the tormenting sense of loneliness within her makes her question herself: "Is this what is then, my life? Only a conundrum that I shall brood over forever with passion and pain, never to arrive at a solution?" (124-25) She commits suicide to escape the "ferocious assaults of existence." (Interview, *Times of India*, 13)

Nirode is another victim of the apathetic and oppressive metropolis of Calcutta. An introvert by nature, he develops an anti-establishment attitude. He is a "congenital failure," a frustrated and rebellious youngman. While returning from the Railway Station after seeing off Arun, who goes abroad for higher studies, Nirode can see his dark future in the blaze of the street light. He visualizes Arun's future as "an undimming brightness." Everybody's love and affection are showered upon Arun, and the brothers and sisters acknowledge his talents. Nirode's inferiority complex leads him to an abyss of misery and self-pity. He wants to live in "shadows, silence and stillness." He works as an anonymous and shabby clerk in a newspaper. He thinks that "three drinks and a room—a princedom" is enough for him. When he achieves this, he gives up his job and starts editing a literary magazine named *Voice.* Then he suddenly changes to writing and when he finds it quite difficult to earn his livelihood he opens a book shop in a dirty locality of Calcutta. Nirode with his friends Sonny, Jit Nair, Dharma and David Gunney represent the bohemian world of Calcutta. They go to the coffee house, "the notorious gathering place of the displaced and dangerous literates of Bengal," to indulge in intellectual debates. Nirode is obsessed with failure but does not regret: "I want to move from failure to failure, step by step to rock bottom." (40) He tells David, "I feel as if I was born with my heart emptied out." (40) His utter sense of loneliness and the life of a social exile impels Nirode to shout: "I am a leper . . . leave me, do not come near. I am a leper, diseased with the loneliest disease of all." (40)

Nirode's repeated failure results in frustration and anguish. It creates in him a longing for loneliness. He himself knows that he is a man for whom "aloneness alone—the treasure worth treasuring." (24) The city of Calcutta seems to him a "dark pandemonium" and on all sides "the city pressed down alight, aglow and stirring with its own marshbred monster life that like an ogre, kept one eye open through sleep and waking." (41) Calcutta pervades over its people like a "living spirit." While returning from the railway platform Nirode feels the "swarming apathy" of Howrah. It is a city of "crass light" which "stung his eyes." In this world of commerce and crowd, he feels life is unfair: "unfair, life is unfair . . . and how faint and senseless it sounded in all that tumult of traffic and commerce about him." (8)

For Amla, Calcutta is a "monstrous city that lived no healthy, red-blooded life." (150) It is a city which "conspires against all who wish to enjoy it." She is a career girl who comes from Bombay to Calcutta after being trained in art to work as a commercial artist with a local firm. She develops a relationship with the portrait painter Dharma, a married man. Amla poses as a model for Dharma's painting. She is a lively girl with "transparent beauty" who attends parties, dinners and dances. Though outwardly she poses to be cheerful, inside, she is as lonely and frustrated as Monisha and Nirode.

When she meets her sister Monisha, she finds "some changes" in her. She feels the monster city of Calcutta "had laid its hand" upon her sister Monisha. She feels that "this monster city that lived no normal, healthy, red-blooded life but one that was subterranean, under-lit, stealthy and odorous of mortality, had captured and enchanted or disenchanted both her sister and brother." (150) She feels the hollowness of life and the futility of existence, despite all the "stimulation of new experiences, new occupations, new acquaintances and mild, sweet winter air, this sense of hollowness and futility persisted." (157) Being fed up by her life in the metropolitan city of Calcutta, Amla repents: "Why ever did I come to Calcutta? Why did not I stay away in Bombay or go home to Kalimpong?" (176-77) Amla's love world shatters to pieces when Dharma disowns his daughter. She was admired by Dharma as a beautiful landscape but now Dharma rejects their joint child: "Dharma was bound by his inhuman act of rejecting their joint child, to shield and protect from further distress and possible insanity." (230-31)

The mother repents for having come away to Kalimpong leaving her children in the city of Calcutta. The city of Calcutta has separated the mother from her children. She repents for not staying at Calcutta and expresses her grief at the rough life her children live in the metropolis, away from her:

> Now I know I made the decisions and changes too abruptly without thinking clearly. Here's Monisha writing such detailed rot about her impossible family—as though she had actually immersed herself in it, or as though it were a theatre to her, I cannot really tell. And Nirode, mute and in exile . . . he must be living a sordid existence, I cannot bear thinking of it. And now Arun's gone from us to his blue eyed Nurse Agnes and they will never come to me as son and daughter. If they come, they will come as strangers. (201-2)

The mother's disinterest in her children is reflected in the city's apathy for its inhabitants. Dharma, Jit, Sonny, Aunt Lila—all the minor characters of the novel are also victims of its indifference.

For Dharma, the city of Calcutta is a dead city. Amla thinks that though it is a dead city it resurges into life like a phoenix every now and then. It takes newcomers into its arms "rough and uncouth as they may be." But for Dharma, there is no sign of a phoenix. The city is dead. It is a city of destruction and demonstration, "the anarchistic genius of Calcutta is intrinsically negative. *Cholbe na* that is the battle cry of all its processions and demonstrations *cholbe na.* It can only end in annihilation." (187) The city has snatched his fifteen-year-old daughter from him who elopes with her first cousin, Dharma's sister's son, a brainless boy of sixteen whom Dharma has brought up like her brother. He tells Amla that he left the city of Calcutta to escape the embarrassment of his daughter's elopement and began living in the suburb of Calcutta. It shows the duality of his attitude—he rejects and accepts the city at the same time.

Calcutta is a city of commerce and, as Jit Nair says, hard drinkers are very much admired in Calcutta. He praises the Calcutta boxwallah in the following words:

> Why is pleasure the most rotten sensation of all in this city? When, where is it to be found clear, fresh, unadulterated? . . . Now I am running down my colleagues again—a pet hobby of the Calcutta boxwallah. . . . Actually I am dedicated to the class. Let me confess, I "belong" to it. They pay me so well, how can I help it? It permits me to indulge in expensive hobbies—expensive for this country at any rate. I owe my imported stereo set to it, and my collection of Rajasthani and Moghul miniatures. (170)

Sonny and his father symbolize the decadent aristocracy of Calcutta. Sonny's father tells Nirode and David about the many splendid things of the past. He presents a beautiful picture of the nautch-girls of Calcutta.

The colour of the city is black, like the colour of Goddess Kali. Like Goddess Kenchamma in Raja Rao's *Kanthapura*, Goddess Kali presides over the city of Calcutta. Goddess Kenchamma provides security and protection to the people but Goddess Kali not only protects the people but also annihilates them: "She is not merely good, she is not merely evil—she is good and evil. . . . The amalgamation of life and death." (256)

Desai deals with the theme of displacement in her third novel *Bye-Bye, Blackbird*. The locale of this novel is London. The city has a strong impact on the sensibilities of the main characters, Dev, Adit and Sarah. The novel opens with the arrival of Dev in London who has the ambition to join the London School of Economics. He secures a job for himself. In spite of it he feels frustrated and develops a hatred for the city because of its ill-treatment of the coloured immigrants. He is horrified by the climate of London. He is also disgusted with the "silence" and "emptiness" of the city. When he arrives in London, he does not get a warm welcome there. On the contrary he comes across various comments on Indians such as "Wogs" and "Macaulay's bastards." The London docks have three kinds of lavatories—Ladies, Gents and Asiatics. A pedlar refuses to tell Dev, the price of a Russian icon, considering him too poor an Indian to buy it. Dev feels insulted. He is drawn inward. He tells Adit that he does not want to live in a country where he is insulted and unwanted. In the city of London, Dev is tortured emotionally. He dreams of an Indian empire where the role of the Indians and the English would be reversed: "Let us abolish the British! Down with Beeching, down with Bradshaw! Let us set up our elephant roots and let the people travel in camel caravans." (63)

Dev is highly critical of the behaviour of the unmarried couple in Hyde park whereas Adit appreciates it. The difference in their reactions to the city reveals the difference in their attitudes. Dev asks Adit: "can you imagine an Indian couple behaving like that?" Adit promptly says, "No, there are not any. Not unmarried ones and the married ones are not in the parks, they are at home quarrelling." (66)

Adit appreciates England because it has given him social and economic freedom. He has married an English girl and adopted British citizenship. He develops a passionate attachment for England. He praises its people and their habits but later on he realizes that he cannot totally shed his Indianness. He is reminded of the colourful festivals like Diwail in India. He feels out of place in England. He tells Sarah that he has been betraying his self so long and he decides to face the reality by going back to India: "All our records and lamb curries and sing songs, it's all so unreal. It has no reality at all. We just pretended all the time. I am twenty seven now. I have got to go home and start living a new life." (204) A peculiar change comes over Dev. His anglophobia changes to an anglophilia. He develops a great fascination for the English people and the English countryside. He begins to wander about London like a tourist. He walks across the streets and parks of the city. He is enchanted by the beautiful daffodils and the bright sunshine. He visits the Lyons Corner House, the Kew Gardens, the Piccadilly circus stand, enjoys the lovely flowers in Mexican boutiques. He visits the British museum. He feels that "it is a strange summer in which he is the bewildered alien, the charmed observer, the out-raged outsider and thrilled sight-seer all at once and in succession." (96)

Dev's newly developed attraction for England creates a dilemma for him so that he cannot decide whether to stay in England or to go back to India. He suffers from what R.S. Sharma calls "Caliban" complex, now adoring, now loathing, the "sensibility that he has imbibed from the colonial rule. Like Caliban, he is trapped within the colonizer's conceptual and operational mode of existence." (39) At last Dev decides: "All I want is—well yes, a good time. Not to return to India, not to marry and breed, go to office, come home and go to office again but—to know a little adventure, to know, to know." (123)

He is intoxicated by the charms of the country. He tells Adit that the streets of London are "an education so rich that he cannot possibly cut it short by entering the stuffy halls of some ancient college." (96)

Dev observes the difference between Indian and British city. In India, cities are "tight, insular, clusters built like fortresses" on plains and sea-coast. The houses, streets, doors, windows everything turn inward in an Indian city. There is no scope to look at the outside. But in London Dev finds "a vista suddenly opening out where he has expected nothing but city." The British people have a very good habit of preserving the old things which shows their respect for the past, whereas the Indian traders are obsessed with the newest. Dev sees the Moradabad brassware and Kashmiri "papier mache" displayed in the market in the Petticoat land. It leads him to think: "Let history turn the table now. Let the Indian traders come to England—the Sikhs and Sindhis with their brass elephant and boxes of spice and tea . . . let them take over the city." (68)

Adit feels homesick. He starts disliking England. The long fingering twilight of the summer seemed to him like an "invalid stricken with anaemia." It creates a desire in him to see again the Indian sunset. Standing in the middle of the busy and crowded Oxford street, Adit eagerly wishes to see a bullock cart or a "monkey wallah." He wishes to see "anything different in colour, tempo, sound, flavour, anything individual and eccentric unruly and unplanned, anything Indian at all." (219) In the chapter *Discovery and Recognition,* Dev discovers that the English country is full of things of interest and recognizes that the English people have a sense of beauty. There is a different type of discovery for Adit. He realizes that his weakness for England is only a pretence and decides to go back to India where his son would be born. The last chapter of the novel depicts the return of the blackbird to its permanent nest.

Sarah lives the life of a cultural exile in her own country. She feels displaced in England by marrying an Indian. She is like Sindhi in Arun Joshi's *Foreigner.* Sindhi is twice removed from his culture and society under circumstantial compulsion. In his opinion, marriage cannot solve the problem of loneliness. Aloneness can be resolved from within. He says to his beloved June: "Marriage would not help June. We are alone, both you and I—that is the problem. And our aloneness must be resolved from within. You cannot send two persons through a ceremony and expect that their aloneness will disappear." Sarah also faces the same problem. Married to an Indian, she tries her best to adjust herself with her Indian husband and his friends. She is worried about the loss of identity in her own society. When people discuss about India, she deliberately avoids the discussion. She is disturbed by an anguish of shedding her own name and identity:

> An anguish it seemed to her of loneliness and then it becomes absurd to call her by her own name—to call her by any name. She had become nameless, she had shed her ancestry and identity and

> she sat there staring, as though she watched them disappear. (*Bye-Bye, Blackbird*, 63)

Sarah is different from Desai's other characters. She is almost an exile in her own land but unlike others she never withdraws. She faces the challenges of life and triumphs over her sufferings and dilemmas. Desai herself says that Sarah's sense of loneliness is very different from her other heroines because she chooses it deliberately whereas for her other characters it is a part of their nature. (Jain, 15)

Sarah is a "silent volcano, not dead yet not bursting." (H. Prasad, 64) Like an existentialist she tries to know her real identity. She questions herself: "who was she—Mrs. Sen who had married in a red and gold Banares brocade Sari one burning bronze day in September, or Mrs. Sen, the Head's Secretary, who sent out the bills and took in the cheques, kept order in the school and was known for her efficiency?" (34) She tries to trace out the real Sarah:

> Where was Sarah? Staring out of the window at the chimneypots and the clouds, she wondered if Sarah had any existence at all, and then she wondered with great sadness, if she would ever be allowed to step off the stage, leave the theatre and enter the real world—whether English or Indian, she did not care, she wanted only its sincerity, its truth. (35)

She feels that the real solution to her problem lies in leaving England and going to India.

The city of Bombay in *Where Shall We Go This Summer?* is a place of violence and destruction where the creative impulse has no chance against the overpowering desire to destroy. Sita is the hypersensitive protagonist of this novel who is a mother of four children and the fifth yet to be born. She escapes from the "madness" of her husband's house to Manori, an island where "it might be possible to be sane again." (35) This escape in reality is an escape from loneliness and boredom that are the two dominant characteristics of city life. The island of Manori symbolizes the pristine world of innocence and purity in contrast to the cannibalistic city of Bombay. In this cannibalistic city, crows form the shadow cabinet. The world of crows in this novel is an extended metaphor for the human world. In the city of alleys and flats there is always much black drama, in this crow theatre "murder, infanticide, incest, theft and robbery, all were much practised by these rough, raucous rasping tatterdemalions." (38) Looking at her bridal photograph in the family album, Sita feels she is no more the shy, graceful bride. The city and its people have left quite a number of scars of experience on it that have changed her into an aggressive, hysteric woman. She turns from the album to the mirror and sees the "layers of experience and melancholy and boredom that had settled upon her face since then like so much grey sand." (54)

After her marriage when Sita comes to Raman's house, she finds herself in a disgusting surrounding. The family members of her husband's house "frighten" her, "appal" her. Her husband Raman, who is neither an extrovert nor an introvert but a "middling kind of man" is unable to gratify her emotional demands. She also suffers from the anguish of failure in communication with her husband, like Maya or Monisha. The lack of understanding on the part of her husband increases her agony. He remains engrossed in his business, her children grow independent and Sita is left alone in the abyss of boredom. But her husband never tries to realize her condition. He thinks everything goes well. He is surprised to hear that Sita is bored:

> Bored? he had exclaimed in genuine surprise why? How? with what? and looked so puzzled so pained. Then it was her turn to be puzzled and pained she could not believe that he had really believed that all was well, not known that she was bored, dull, unhappy, frantic. She could hardly believe that though they lived so close together, he did not even know this basic fact of her existence. (144-45)

The evils of the city are manifest in the nature and behaviour of the family members. Sita remembers the first years of their marriage, with Raman's family in their "age-rotted flat" of Queens Road. In her husband's house she revolts against their "subhuman placidity," "calmness" and "sluggishness." Frantic with fear he fears that their subhumanity might swamp her. (48) She behaves provocatively, starts smoking and begins to speak in "sudden rushes of emotion as though flinging darts at their smooth, unscarred faces." (48) Sita takes to smoking instead of eating and the family members of Raman's house seem to her "nothing but sex and appetite." (49) She spends almost all her time standing in the balcony and smoking. After some days Raman and Sita move to a small flat with their children. But here also she does not find an amicable surrounding. The vegetarian "complacence" and "solidity" of the people who interfere and intrude upon her privacy, infuriate her.

A woman in her forties, Sita is pregnant. Maddened by the boredom and loneliness of her life in the city of Bombay, she wants to go back to her father's island. Her decision to go there is to abandon the turmoil of the city of Bombay. Raman considers her decision to go back to Manori to be no more than sheer madness for in the island she would not find any doctor or hospital or telephone. But she tells her husband that she wants to escape to the island from the madness of the present surrounding. She wants to escape to a place where "it might be possible to be sane again." (35)

The city has a powerful impact on the children and all its inhabitants. The children see violence in the films and fight with each other. The ayahs take the babies to the road-side and let them play in the dust as they themselves indulge in gossip. Sita wants to avoid all these and wants to go to the island where she thinks "it will be different." She wants to keep her child unborn for she does not want to see another violent act by giving birth to the child. Her two children Menaka and Karan frighten her by their behaviour. Sita watches disbelievingly at Menaka when she crumbles a sheaf of new buds or tears off her paintings. Sita is unable to bear the sight of such "unthinking destruction." She is appalled to see destruction coming so naturally to the children. Karan builds a tower of blocks only for the "pure, lustful joy of throwing it over with a great clatter, so much more enjoying the downfall than the architecture." (45-46) She finds in the city and in her people no desire to destroy: "The creative impulse has no chance against the overpowering desire to destroy." (46)

Coming back to Manori, Sita finds that the island has also been affected by the passage of time during the last twenty five years. It no longer remains the idealized island of Sita's childhood. It is in a dilapidated and rundown condition. Karan and Menaka insist on going back to the urbanized life and Sita has to compromise with her children. Menaka invites her father to take them back to Bombay, as she has to apply for admission to the medical college. Looking at the "unbearable excitement" of her children at the arrival of Raman, she feels that "they are being disloyal to her, disloyal to the island and its wild nature." (129) She realizes that by escaping to the island she has escaped "from duties, from responsibilities, from order and routine from life and the city, to unlivable island." (139) She comes to the understanding that "Life must be continued, and all its business—Menaka's admission to medical college gained, wife led to hospital, new child safely brought forth, the children reared, a salary earned, a salary spent." (138) She realizes that the only solution to all existential problems is to "only connect." Sita's loneliness is symbolic of the loneliness of "a woman, a wife, a mother—the loneliness conditioned by familial and social constraints." (Asnani, *Indian Literature*, 198) She accepts the grim truth that she has to face the assaults of existence all alone.

Nanda Kaul, the protagonist of *Fire on the Mountain* earnestly longs for loneliness as an escape from her busy and hectic life in the city. She comes to Carignano where "she wanted no one and nothing else whatever else comes or happened here would be an unwelcome intrusion and distraction." (3) It is the place and the time of life that "she has wanted and prepared for all her life" and at last she gets it. She keeps herself "religiously aloof" being jealous of "this privacy achieved only at the end of her life." (35-36) As the Vice-Chancellor's wife and the centre of a large family Nanda spends a life of duties and responsibilities ordering about "too many servants," entertaining "too many guests" and tending "so many children." The crowd of the house, full of guests and people, stifle her and consequently, she suffers from the "nimiety, disorder, the fluctuating and unpredictable excess." (30) After the death of her husband, Nanda vacates the Vice-Chancellor's house and comes over to Kasauli. She identifies herself with the lonely pine tree. She likes the 'bareness,' the 'emptiness' of the garden of Carignano.

The first intrusion that comes into her sequestered life is the postman's letter informing her that Tara's daughter Raka, her great grandchild, who "looks like a ghost" and "who has not quite got over her typhoid yet" will come to spend her holidays at Carignano. The letter comes as a threat to Nanda Kaul, as if Raka would bring her back to her past, to the life in the city. She receives the letter from the postman and thanks him "in a voice of suffering." (12) When Raka arrives, Nanda Kaul thinks her as "an intruder, an outsider, a mosquito flown up from the plains to tease and weary." (40) But one day she discovers that Raka is not like other children but basically a child of loneliness who only wants "to be left alone and pursue her own secret life amongst rocks and pines of Kasauli." (47-48) Nanda Kaul feels that Raka is exactly like her.

Carignano is presented in this novel as a contrast to the life of the city. Nanda Kaul's dislike for the city life results in her escape to Carignano. She has no interest in the big family that she has to manage or to be the Vice-Chancellor's wife simply to entertain guests. Asha, in her letter to Nanda, mentions about the heat of Delhi and the duststorm in summer. Asha thinks it would be very nice for Raka's health to stay at Carignano for the speedy recovery of her health and the "heat and humidity of Bombay will do her no good." (15)

The novel *Clear Light of Day* begins with Tara's visit with her husband Bakul to Bim who stays in Old Delhi, where "everything goes on and on and never changes." (4) Whatever happened here, had happened long ago during the time of the Tughlaqs, the Khiljis, the Sultanate or the Moghuls. Bim, the elder sister, still a spinster, works as a lecturer in a private college. She has sacrificed her own happiness for the sake of her old aunt and retarded brother Baba. When Raja was sick, Bim had taken great care of him with the hope that he would look after the family when he would recover. But Raja turns his back on Bim and goes to Hyderabad after his marriage with Hyder Ali's daughter and finally settles there. Bim is left "alone in the house with Baba to brood over."

Bim consoles Baba that though everybody has left them they will not be alone. The realization comes to her as she reads *The Life of Aurangzeb* one night: "'Many were around me when I was born but now I am going alone" and "strange that I come with nothing into the world, and now go away with this stupendous caravan of Sin." (167) These lines fill her eyes with tears. She tears off all the old papers and makes herself free from the debris of past. She is now in a mood to forgive Raja.

The city of Delhi remains behind the scene and displays its ugly nature through the ingratitude, lack of feelings and cruelty of the characters, Bim is the victim of all these. Bim relates to Tara the boredom and her anguish of loneliness in the city of Delhi. Old Delhi is a symbol of monotony and decay: "That is the risk of coming home to Old Delhi. Old Delhi does not change. It only decays. My students tell me it is a great cemetery, every house is a tomb. Nothing but sleeping graves." (5) When Tara refuses to go with Bakul to his uncle's place in New Delhi, he gets annoyed with her:

> So I only have to bring you home for a day Tara, and you go back to being the hopeless person you were before I married you. And you won't let me help you. I thought I had taught you a different life, different way of living. Taught you to execute your will. Be strong. Face challenges. Be decisive. But no, the day you enter your old home, you are as weak-willed and helpless and defeatist as ever. (17)

Thus Tara becomes a part of Old Delhi, and the old house of her childhood. She is not prepared to accept the changing pattern of time, she rather makes futile attempts to cling to the memories of her childhood. The Misra family is a symbol of the decadence of values that Old Delhi symbolizes. The two grey-haired, spectacled daughters of the Misras are married and both rejected by their husbands. They run a nursery school in the day and give song and dance lessons during evening to support their old father and three grown up brothers who sit idle. The brothers are drunkards and obese. They drink whisky and arrange soirees which they can hardly afford. The old Misra tells Bim that both she and his daughters are alike. They undergo suffering for the happiness of others: "You and my girls—you are too alike—you work and let the brothers enjoy. Look at my sons there. Look at my sons. Look at them—fat, lazy slobs, drinking whisky. Drinking whisky all day that their sisters have to pay for—did you ever hear of such a thing?" (32) He remembers his young days when he was even worse than them, a "boozer, a womaniser, a bankrupt—running after drink, women, money—that was all I did just like them, worse than them, any of them." (34)

The novel also deals with the partition riots of 1947 when the whole city was in flames. During this Hyder Ali's family leave Delhi and go to Hyderabad. When Raja knows about it he becomes worried. Then he decides to go to Hyderabad, "I won't stop with you, another day. It's enough—enough." (95) After going to the city of Hyderabad, Raja changes his role from a brother to a landlord, because of his marriage with Hyder Ali's daughter. The city brings about a change in his nature. The story of Aunt Mira is really tragic. A widow at a tender age she comes to take care of the children—Bim, Tara, Raja and Baba. She suffers from a terrible disease. She takes to alcohol and at last dies a tragic death.

A change comes over Bim, when she attends the musical soiree arranged by the Misras where Mulk's guru sings. She perceives a contrast between Mulk's "sweet and clear voice" and his guru's "sharp voice" mingled with "bitterness," "sadness," "passion" and "frustration" which lead her to think that both of them "belonged to the same school." She comes to realize the significance of time in relation to eternity. She realizes that time is both the destroyer and the preserver. Thus the 'house' that contains all the memories of the past becomes a part of eternity: "That soil contained all time, past and future, in it. It was dark with time, rich with time. It was here where her deepest self lived, and the deepest selves of her sister and brothers and all those who shared that time with her." (182)

The city of Mirpore is a "cruel trap," an "indestructible prison" for the protagonist Deven, in Desai's novel, *In Custody*. Deven works as a lecturer in a private college in this small town. His childhood friend Murad comes from the metropolis of Delhi to meet him and to ask him to take an interview of the great poet Nur. He wishes to publish this interview in his magazine. When the offer comes from Murad to go to Delhi, Deven at once agrees. The small town of Mirpore lacks history and probably "it existed for centuries in its most basic, most elemental form." (19) The roads are covered with tar but the dust is still present under them. During the monsoon it becomes muddy. The inhabitants are mostly petty businessmen rather than agriculturists. People have no respect for the historical monuments: the small mosque of marble and sandstone which was built by a nawab who had escaped from Delhi after the mutiny of 1857 and lived in this small town. It has become disfigured because of the invasion of urban life into this small town. The white marble-facing has turned "grey and pock-marked" due to "urban pollution." The red sandstone had turned to the colour of filth from "the smoke of open fires, the excreta of pigeons and the ubiquitous dust of Mirpore." (20) Mirpore is full of numerous temples which have many legends but no history at all.

A sense of vacuum pervades over the entire town. There is no river in Mirpore. There is only an artificial tank that supplies people with water for both drinking and bathing. The water in this tank is so scant that "bits of papers, rags, flowers" are only visible. There are also wells in this city, but "the water was even more successfully concealed" in them. The people live in the bazars which are joined and separated by different religious groups.

There are also violence and disturbance in this "shapeless, formless town." The town is full of mosques, temples, shops and cinema houses. It has flowerbeds which contain only empty tins and paper bags but no flowers. Mirpore is isolated but not cut off from the mainland. The city of Mirpore is full of sounds but the sounds are unproductive, "there were really more of bustle than doldrums and it was deafening." (23)

The "solidity and stubbornness" of the town have formed a trap for Deven. The distance between Mirpore and Delhi being very short, the town has lost its idyllic beauty and has been pervasively infected by the urban milieu of neighbouring Delhi. The fields look withered and desolate, the atmosphere is filled with smoke. Different factories have been set up. When Deven completes his study, gets married and comes to Mirpore, he finds it an "impassable desert that lay between him and the capital with its lost treasures of friendships, entertainment, attractions and opportunities. It turned into that strip of no-man's land that lies around a prison, threatening in its desolation." (24)

The city of Delhi is the "polluting honeycomb of commerce," in which Deven fears "we must be lost." It is "as gloomy as a prison." Except for its "colour" and "noise" Chandni Chowk might have been "a bazar encountered in a nightmare." (36) It is like a 'maze' from which there is no exit. The 'heat' and the 'crowd' of this place "pressed down from above and all sides, solid and suffocating as sleep." (36) The bazar is full of colourful things. The sherbets in the shop are "poison green" and "red." The varieties of sarees in the show cases of the shops look like "gaudy but shimmering prostitutes propositioning the passers by." There are astrologers and palmists and "soothsayers" who spread the exotic tools of their trade. The "tea shop" is a symbol of the unhygienic and uncouth life of the city people. Deven finds a dead fly floating in the tea cup when he drinks it. The slow atmosphere around the shop gives the idea of the "wretched standards of hygiene" in the shop. There is the fear of infectious diseases in this area. The insecurity, the sound, the filth and violence that pervade over the entire metropolis lead Deven to reflect: "What madness had drawn him out to undertake this journey into what could only be disaster." (27)

Deven arrives at the house of the great poet Nur. To his great disappointment, he finds the poet of his dream in a pitiable condition, surrounded by shopkeepers, louts who do not have any artistic taste for art. Sitting in Nur's house and waiting for him, Deven observes the city life outside which seems to have encroached upon the life of the poet. Though a large number of people come out of and go into the room, no one pays any attention to the poet. The terrace is filled with people and the house looks like a "public park" on a "promenade" to which these people are "accustomed to repair" at this time when the city's sky is blotched with the city's "soot" and fades to "grey and then to mauve and finally to an uneasy, disturbed darkness." (49) The shops and cinema houses are lit up for the night and the sky is tinged with different colours, such as red, orange, yellow and violet like "an old hag at a fair crazily dancing a dance of seven veils." (49) The cacophonous noise of the street and the traffic increases and it mixes up with the blaring song coming out of the cinema hall at the end of the street. The roof-top "did not really raise one above the din of the streets, it was as if they were inside a balloon floating above but remaining enclosed." (50) Coming back to his own house at Mirpore after interviewing Nur, Deven feels relieved of all tensions. He thinks it a "vain-glory to try to find an entry into Nur's world." All that Nur could measure up was "this shabby house, its dirty corners, its wretchedness and lovelessness." (67) Being persuaded by Murad he again goes to Delhi to record Nur's voice in a tape recorder. Gradually Deven is entrapped in Nur's world. His poetry also becomes a trap for Deven. His trip to Delhi teaches him a great deal about the relationship between art and human nature. He learns from his encounter with Imtiaaz-Begum that art can survive gloriously even in brothel house. The city of Delhi sadly lacks the "the bliss of solitude," which as Wordsworth would have us believe, is the basic condition of the creative process. In the metropolis, silence is a dream. It turns a great poet like Nur hungry and desolate. The apathy and insensibility of the city and its people towards art and artist lead Deven to ponder over the condition of the artist in the city. "How can the intellectuals of this country do any worthwhile work if no one shows them any respect or compensates them for all the suffering they have to undergo for the sake of art?" (14)

"Accepting—not accepted" is the story of Hugo Baumgartner's life. A wandering Jew all his life, his complexion was too dark for Germany that had marked him the "Jewder Jude" and in India he was too fair and that branded him as the "firanghi." In both lands, he was "the unacceptable." (20) The sense of loneliness was deeply rooted in Baumgartner. He grew up as a lonely child and an isolated youth. Berlin, where he spent his childhood and a fairly large part of his youth was increasingly unsafe and when he came to India he remained a solitary foreigner.

Apart from Baumgartner's inherent sense of loneliness, the city and the people further accentuate his sense of loneliness. In Calcutta he stays in a hotel in Middleton Row which looks like a substantial villa. The city manifests its ugliness through its different facets—the prostitutes, the mosquitoes, the heat of the sun and the noise of the crowd.

Baumgartner feels suffocated in the streets of Calcutta. He finds no joy in the streets where he walks aimlessly and compulsively: "The congestion of the streets and the odours in the heat were overpowering, debris was piled everywhere—banana peels, coconut husks, ashes and cinders from the fires, the householders lit in their small brick stones in kerosenes, a lethal substance that let out billows of choking yellow smoke." (172)

The house where Baumgartner stays is surrounded by other inhabitants—the rickshaw pullers, prostitutes, daily labourers, drunkards etc. The sounds of metal pots, typewriters, thrashing and beating of wives by the drunkards further accentuate the devilish aspect of place. The city has no charm for Baumgartner. He is totally disgusted the day he finds Sushil, the boy who always listens to the radio is brutally murdered. He has a nightmarish experience when he sees the blood of Sushil. To him it seems to be the blood of his Mutti: "In his sleep, in his dreams the blood was Mutti's not the boy's. Yet his mother so small, weak could not have split so much blood or had she? The blood ran, ran over the floor and down the stairs, soaking his feet which stood in it helplessly." (179)

If Baumgartner is a victim of the apathetic and malignant influence of the city, Lotte is a co-sufferer of no less intensity. After coming to India she gets married to Kantisethia, a businessman with a wife and children. He keeps Lotte in a different house and visits her occasionally when he gets tired and is in need of a change. Like Baumgartner, she is also an exile in the city of Bombay: "mostly I am alone. All, all alone." (203)

In India, Baumgartner finds only Lotte who belonged to the India of his own experience. They find each other comfortable as brother and sister together. With other Europeans he tries to maintain a distance. He does not like to reveal his identity, his background and therefore does not like their "probing questions, their determination to discover his background, his circumstances, his past, and present and future, before they accepted him." (150)

Baumgartner does not know why he should be so secretive about his circumstances, yet a fastidiousness about his private affairs makes him secretive and he wants to reveal everything to someone who can take the entire thing to be granted. He has no intention to go back to his country because "Germany when flourished had not wanted him and Germany destroyed would have no need of him either." (167) So he comes to Bombay, keeping in mind Habibullah's words: "Bombay had no war, no famine where no one stabs at the back, a great city."

But the city and its inhabitants deeply hurt him by their apathy that isolated him as a foreigner. The behaviour of Chimanlal's sons and others at the cremation of Chimanlal is one such incident which touches him deeply:

> all of whom shrank away from him, horrified by the presence of a foreigner, a 'firanghi' at such an intensely private rite. Hearing the babbling chant of the priests, seeking the confusion around the pyre, smelling the odours of burnt flesh and charred wood under the noontime sun, Baumgartner too wished he had not come, and shuffled away. (206).

Though Baumgartner lives in Bombay for thirty years yet he has failed to enter into its real life. The city too has failed to understand him: "The life of Bombay which had been Baumgartner's life for thirty years now—or rather, the setting for his life, he had never actually entered it, never quite captured it, damply, odorously cacophonously palpable as it was, it had been elusive still." (214) Thus the city has destroyed Baumgartner's peace of mind. He has been betrayed by his own country. He is even betrayed to death by Kurt, the boy whom he gives shelter under his own roof.

In spite of its indifference, filth, dust, noise and crowd, the city becomes an inescapable part of the artist's perceptions and vision. Desai portrays "the present crisis of man" and the "enduring human conditions" (178) in the perspective of the urban metropolis. As no man's life is an island, man has to exist in society amidst all troubles, pain and suffering. The problem before him is "how to exist" and not "how to exit."

As Desai herself asserts:

> Personally I do not think anybody's exile from society can solve any problem. I think basically the problem is how to exist in society and yet maintain one's individuality rather than suffering from a lack of society and a lack of belonging, that is why exile has never been my theme. ("Interview," *Stairs to the Attic*, 15)

The novels of Anita Desai reflect an acute awareness of the city in its multiple diversions of agony and ecstasy and embody an ambivalent vision of hope and despair, rejection and acceptance in terms of the metaphors drawn from the urban ethos.

The Ironic Presence: Nature and Spirit

Nature plays a significant role in Anita Desai's fiction. In the stark, barren and lifeless lives of the protagonists Nature acts both as a metaphor of hope and life and as an ironical presence that sharpens the awareness of a grim existence in the hollow metropolis. Desai's perception of the city is deeply interfused with a subtle awareness of Nature in all its diversity—the flower and the grass, the seasons and the hills, the animals and the birds. While Desai's perception of Nature is in itself quite delightful, Nature also provides a symbolic dimension to the total meaning of her fiction and thus becomes a shaping element of her form and style. Nature in Anita Desai's novels appears basically in its two perspectives: (a) as tamed and enclosed, perceived through the metaphor of the garden and (b) as open and benign, perceived through sights and sounds.

"I was drawn away from pain into a world that knew no pain," (*Cry the Peacock*, 21) says the morbid and morose Maya in the presence of the flowers in the garden. Her sad mood mingles with the mood of the flowers as she inhales their scent: "I bent upon them, inhaling that mist of sad maidenly scent feeling mood merge into mood, sensation into sensation, till there was nothing left but that mist." (21)

The spring season comes with the long insistent call of the brain fever bird. The spring is combined with the qualities of the autumn as the trees shed their leaves and new leaves about to appear in them. The silk cotton trees are first to flower, "their huge, scarlet blooms, thick petalled solid podded, that made blood-blobs in the blue." (34) The spring in her garden reminds Maya of another spring—the spring of her childhood which was "far more idyllic one" (36) when she had been strolling amidst the vegetables with her father. The paradisal state of innocence of the garden of her childhood is glorified by Maya when she remembers the breakfast in the garden wlth her father which was like a feast or a revel of the elves and fairies who "feast on melons and syrups by moonlight." The garden has an element of fantasy attached to it. Maya remembers: "Our table is laid beside a mandarine orange tree there is one in each corner of the garden a little faery tree, with its glossy leaves, and an overload of small, bright miniature lanterns on a carnival night." (44) When Sapru's wife comes to the garden with her loose, straggling hair, sobs and complains against the irresponsibility of her husband, Maya's father feels agitated. He says to Maya, "it is remarkable what a magnet human nature can be for disorder and failure." (45) He cannot tolerate disorder of any sort. He is a man of orderliness, and is systematic like a Moghul garden, "gracious and exact where breeding, culture, leisure and comfort have been brought to a nice art." (45)

The garden of Maya's childhood and the garden at present intermingle as the flow of thoughts cascade down from past to present. Her memory stretches towards the single white blossom outside her room, and the garden strikes her as a symbol of symmetry, pattern and order that are absent in her own life. She finds these values in her father's character and also in the lives of other people, her neighbours whose gardens are well protected whereas her own garden has been neglected. She goes upstairs to the roof and gazes into her own little garden, leaning over the parapet. She also gazes at the gardens of others and searches for a pattern and a design that has "deserted her own life." She soon realizes she has failed to take care of her garden: "I have failed to care for my garden for so long now, and the gardener has neglected it." (180)

In Maya's garden of Eden, the snake enters in the guise of the albino astrologer. Maya lies in her chair waiting for somebody she does not know: "I lay back in my chair and breathed deeply, lay there waiting for summer? for snakes? for the moon? I did not know." (12) She has the vision of the snake in the form of a "giant physical shadow," the shadow of the astrologer and his prophecy. She feels as if in the thick blades of grass, the snake reaches her, lapping her feet. She leaps from her chair in terror "overcome by a sensation of snakes coiling and uncoiling their moist length about me, of evil descending from an overhanging branch of an insane death, unprepared for heralded by deafening drum beats." (13) The seasonal flowers are not there but there are still some beds of petunias which are "sentimental, irresolute flowers" which emanate fragrance that matches her mood to perfection and she stares at them "with the embrace of recognition." (19)

The garden of Kalimpong is Monisha's abode of peace into which she escapes through memory to forget the violence, the crowd and lack of privacy in the city of Calcutta. She experiences a deathlike stillness in the city and most of the time she thinks about Kalimpong and about Jiban's last posting in a district away from the city and the family. She is delighted by the solitude of the jungles: "the acqueous shadows of the bamboo groves and the earth led with great fallen leaves." (*Voices in the City*, 116)

In her letter, Monisha's mother refers to the profusion of spring in the garden of Kalimpong. Monisha's dull existence in the house and the lack of any communication with others drive her towards an inner garden, a garden of her own creation. Amla reflects: "This sister had wandered away, into some unholy garden of her own, stood there now like one of those lifeless statues, on the brink of the stone fountain was dry and what confronted her was no ripple and tickle of cool water but only dry hard flagstones." (149) Aunt Lila's garden is sharply contrasted with the garden of Kalimpong. The "bird of paradise" has long flown from this garden. It is a "dark, unbreathing garden" where "unmown grass housed singing swarms of mosquitoes and spider webs alone multiplied and reproduced amidst the leaves of the plantains and mango trees that had years ago surrendered the desire to propagate and fructify." (148)

Dharma's paintings seem to be the "studies of the finer secrets of nature." Looking at the still pond where the white geese swim silently, Dharma says to Nirode: "So it has, Nirode, like you, I find myself inexorably drawn away from my island back to the mainland again." (224)

Nature acts as the agent of change in the taste and attitude of Dev. His strong resentment turns to appreciation as he wanders through London enjoying its natural scenery. The beautiful daffodils in the parks, the patches of bright sunshine, the grass under the green canopies of the Kew Garden have a great impact on him. He is intoxicated by the beauty of the countryside. The fields of tall, ripe hay and wheat and barely swaying in the gentle breeze look luxuriantly green and golden. There is no speck of dust, no patch of arid earth, no sign of blight" (*Bye-Bye, Blackbird*, 126) for miles together.

The island of Manori with the vast smooth sea all around it, symbolizes Sita's lonely life amidst her own family and the society. The sea is "silk-smooth" which bounds with enthusiasm and sparkles with hope. But the island concretizes Sita's feeling of isolation. It "primarily exists in its full reality" only in her mind and no more than a "projection of her inner psyche," says Vimala Rao. (46) Nature thus presented through the metaphor of the island is closed and cut off from all outside relationships. But presented through the sea it is open, benign and wide. The sea stands between the two polarities of the city and the island. As R.S. Sharma aptly observes if the city is symbolic of a "rational way" of life, the island becomes symbolic of "the primitive reality." (*Commonwealth Quarterly*, 55) Sita's return to the island suggests both renewal and regeneration as well as alienation. To the island where Sita's father had created a distinct social identity for himself and his followers, Sita comes back in search of her personal identity.

The final section of the novel *Where Shall We Go This Summer?* presents Nature in its colourful variety. The description of the monsoon is indeed lyrical:

> The monsoon flowed—now thin, now dense; now slow, now fast; now whispering, now drumming; then gusting. There was never silence—always the roar and sign of tide, the moan of casuarinas in the grove below, tossed and hurled about in grey, tattered billows, the clatter of palm leaves that hung their ragged fingers down and made channels for the rain to spout down onto the roof. (102)

Nature provides joy, but it is also an ironical reminder of the grim realities of life. Sita tries her best to forget her sorrow and agony in the island of Manori but the rain persistently revives her memory: "Usually she repressed them with an agonized determination but the rain drumming, thrumming, pouring all about her locked her in, locked her up, forced her to turn on herself." (112)

As the monsoon breaks Sita and her children stand on the terrace to watch the clouds. The clouds are "Kohl-black floating and shifting and casting a shadow over the 'slaty sea' changing it into green-black colour. A shaft of white sunlight is reflected upon the dancing waves of the sea. The clouds remain loose and buoyant. From the terrace Sita and her children watch the sails move in and out of the islands of light.

Sea and water are two dominant symbols in *Where Shall We Go This Summer?* In the presence of the island and the sea Sita never feels alone: "She never felt alone. She felt surrounded by presences—the presence of the island itself, of the sea around it and of the palm trees that spoke to each other and, sometimes, even to her. They were so alive." (126) Sita discovers, in the sea, the ultimate intangibility of life. She identifies herself with the jelly fish stranded on the sand bar "washed up by the waves." Sita feels: "Perhaps I am only the jelly fish washed up by the waves, stranded there on the sand-bar. I was just stranded here by the sea, that's all. I had not much to do with it all she sadly admitted, with that black, stripped truthfulness that she could never colour or coat." (152) After her reconciliation with Raman, she realizes that "her time on the island had been very much of an episode on a stage" (152) and that she must go back to her routine life of duties and responsibilities.

Nanda Kaul, the protagonist of *Fire on the Mountain* moves away from the mainland and is drawn back to the hills of Carignano for privacy, solitude and tranquillity. As the Vice-Chancellor's wife and the head of a large family she had a hectic and disturbed life. She had longed for privacy all through her life and at last got it in the hills of Kasauli: "Here on the ridge of the mountains in this quiet house. It was the place and the time of life, that she had wanted and prepared for all her life—as she realized on her first day at Carignano, with a great, cool flowering of relief and at last she had it. She wanted no one and nothing else." (3) The garden of Carignano is a projection of Nanda Kaul's yearning for loneliness and privacy. The fresh fragrance of the flowers refreshes her as she walks across the lawn. She enjoys the sight of the phlox bloomed in a border edging the lawn. They are close, white and fresh giving out a scent of "freshness and cool." The garden of Carignano is also a projection of Nanda Kaul's self that is bare and empty. She does not wish to plant a tree in it like any other owner but enjoys its bareness. The garden is as lonely as its owner: "No she revelled in its bareness, its emptiness. The loose pebbles of the garden pleased her as much as rich turf might another. She cared not to add another tree to the group of apricots by the verandas or the group of three pines at the gate." (31)

Through age and experience the garden has arrived at a state of elegance and perfection like Nanda Kaul. The garden is exact and beautiful in its present state and needs no addition. It is made of a very few elements but they are exact and "germane as the strokes in a Japanese scroll." (31) Nanda Kaul does not want any addition to it as she does not wish to add to her own "pared, reduced and radiantly single life." (31) She thinks Raka is an intruder "a mosquito flown up from the plains to tease and weary." (39) Looking at her Raka thinks of Nanda as another pine tree. Her grey saree, a rock, "all components of the bareness and stillness of garden." (40) Nanda Kaul is surprised to discover that Raka has the gift of disappearing suddenly and silently for hours together. She finds Raka the "perfect model" of what she herself is—merely a "brave, flawed experiment." If Nanda is a "recluse of vengeance," her great grandchild Raka is a recluse by "nature, by instinct." Raka is "born to it simply." (48) Solitude never disturbs her. She never asks for anything. She is very different from other children. She has come to Carignano for nothing else but to be alone, "stubbornly to be alone." Her intense love for Carignano makes Nanda think that Carignano belongs to none else but to Raka: "Certainly it belonged to no one else, had no meaning for anyone else. Raka alone understood Carignano, she alone valued that, Nanda Kaul knew." (80)

Coming home, Tara in *Clear Light of Day* finds the garden of her childhood neglected and abandoned. The rose walk is a strip of grass, still streaked green and grey which lies between two beds of roses at the end of the lawn. There is a line of trees like silver oak, mulberry and eucalyptus at this place of the garden. Tara thinks probably this is the only place where "bit of cultivation left" everything else, even the papaya and lilies seemed abandoned to dust and to neglect, to struggle as they could against the heat and sun of summer." (1)

The rose walk takes Tara back to her childhood. She remembers how as a child she has followed her mother to the garden when her mother was expecting her last child and was advised by the doctor to take some exercise. Tara while walking beside her mother used to scream at the sight of a snail in the garden. Now as she shouts at the sight of a snail, Bim is surprised to see "a grown up woman" playing with a snail. Through the snail, Tara tries to capture the feelings and experiences of her childhood. Her reluctance to accept the passage of time is further reinforced by the image of the monotonous sound produced by the coppersmiths beating on the metal in the sleeping garden symbolizing the fleeting Time: "In the sleeping garden the coppersmiths beat on and on monotonously like mechanics at work on a metal sheet tonk, tonk, tonk. Tonk, tonk, tonk." (23) Their garden is neglected like those of their neighbours which are also "still, faded and shabby as theirs." These gardens are overgrown and teemed with "wild, uncontrolled life." (34) But in the garden of Hyder Ali there are roses of different variety. Tara wonders, "Why could they not have such roses too."

Thus in Desai's novels garden signifies privacy, security and pattern. It is polarized against the city which stands for human vulnerability, insecurity and violence. In the chaotic and ambivalent world of the protagonists it is the only benign presence which seeks to strike a harmony between the past and the present. It symbolizes the soothing experiences of the past as well as the unhappy predicament of the present. It is in this respect that the garden becomes an integral part of the form of Desai's fiction.

A sense of insecurity, horror and bareness pervades the landscape of Delhi in the novel *In Custody*. When Deven comes to Delhi for an interview with the poet Nur, he perceives the landscape of Delhi in terms of "white dust and yellow weeds, the leafless thorn trees, the broken fences, isolated tin and brick shacks and the scattered carcasses of cattle that littered the landscape and yet rendered it more bleak and more bare under the empty sky." (27)

The neem tree which has grown outside the wall of Deven's house has branches spreading out to the courtyard. Deven's wife Sarala wants the branches to be cut down as they keep out the sun, but Deven forbids her to do so as the tree gives them shade during summer. Deven feels caged by marriage, family and job. He spends the life of a prisoner and does not find freedom anywhere. He looks up at the sky to find out some chink that could promise or assure an escape from his present state of existence. But Nature does not provide him any solace. He finds the stars "smothered and murk." They do not promise any hope. The "nocturnal breeze" brings no message. The leaves of the neem tree are dry, still and lifeless. The starkness and lifelessness in nature reflect the drab and unexciting nature of life: "Out in the lane a bullock cart creaked by the wooden wheels lacking oil and shrieking dismally. Across the canal a stray dog barked in a long monotonous howl of protest. Then there was silence. A long while later it was broken by the sharp shrill whistle of the Janata Express from Assam clattering down the railway line." (131-32)

When Deven visits Delhi again in the summer he finds the entire plain laid waste by "months of devastating heat." There is nothing to see except the "sulphur yellow dust." There is not a single crow or vulture to be seen. He observes: "Bushes and grass all appeared to have died; the land was shorn, or shrouded." (187)

The starkness and bareness in Nature correspond to the pattern of life the protagonists lead. In Anita Desai's novels the trees, birds, seasons, hills and gardens symbolize hope, regeneration and freshness as well as the grim reality of existence.

Nature in Anita Desai's fiction plays an important role in shaping the spirits of the protagonists. Violence, murder, madness also occur in the world of Nature. Through its different moods and elements Nature casts a deep shadow over the spirits of these characters who are but helpless victims of a cruel, indifferent and malignant Nature. The elements of violence in Nature are presented through different sights and sounds.

Amidst the flowers and trees in the garden, under the starry night, Maya is conscious of some evil, an indefinable unease. She feels the presence of a "truly physical shadow" like the shadow of a giant tree approaching her, spilting across the leaves and grasses. She feels snakes coiling and uncoiling and lapping at her feet. It is the figure of the astrologer in her subconscious and his prophecy which has been revived in her memory by the death of her pet dog Toto. Maya anticipates another tragedy about to happen.

The blossoms of the lemon tree are stronger, crisper as if the petals are cut out of "hard moon shells" by a sharp knife of mother-of-pearl into curving, scimitar petals "that guarded the heart of fragrance." (*Cry, the Peacock*, 19) But the fragrance and the flowers have no meaning for Gautama. He has always shrugged off Maya's words as superfluous and trivial. Instead of the flowers, Gautama looks at the night sky. Maya sees the stars surging towards them. The stars are bright. They symbolize hope. But in the midst of their shining beauty, Maya is also conscious of the "still spaces of darkness" above and around them. She feels as if Death is lurking in these spaces. The darkness speaks about the "distance, separation and loneliness." Maya is drawn inward to herself, to her own situations. The sky looks intensely black and soft. The deep dark night always looks beautiful. Maya smells a "foreign odour" amidst the scent of the lemon blossoms. She stretches for the stars unhappily, fearsomely as if they communicate an important message to her in a language which she cannot read, "it was as though I were faced with an important message in a language I could not read." (27)

The message comes at last; not through the stars but through the moon. The moon, vast and "ghost white" casts a shearing shaft of "stark white" over Maya's body. The moon is not the benevolent moon of the love ballads and fairy revels but a fearful moon "demoniac creature," "the fiercer dancer," the "mad demon" of the Kathakali dancer heavily masked with skirts swirling and stamping his feet and with eyes shooting "beams of fire." The moon brings to Maya's mind the sound of defeaning drum beats as if "it was a phantom gone berserk." (28)

The spring season begins with the mournful cry of the brain fever bird upsetting Maya violently. It is the spring in Gautama's garden in the metropolis of Delhi which makes her sad and insomniac. In contrast to this, the spring of Maya's memory, the idyllic spring of her childhood is quite different. The spring in her father's garden is full of blossoms in their colourful variety. She sees through them the sky and the vast lawn stretching out towards the creeper-hung bungalow. The garden is full of butterfly, grass, green foliage and flowers. The bare neem tree very carefully conceals the nests of the birds and children throw stones at them. They send pariah kites high up to the sky that pale from the cold weather's intense cobalt to an "effete milk washed blue." Children pick up the radiant billows of the pods of the cotton tree and blow them up in the air and women collect them to sell to the manufacturers of pillows and babies's quilts. The pigeon's nests on the verandah are filled with babies who twitter and mutter all day.

The loneliness and insanity in Maya are suggested through several images taken from Nature—the wind, the dust storm, the snake, iguanas and the desert. Maya remembers the beautiful white flowers like tuberose and queen of Night. But all these chaste white flowers lure snakes to their "hearts of scent." The snakes come slithering towards these "virgins of the night" and with their forked tongues "lash and lash again at the heart of innocence." (126) The rats, with their young suckling them, also spread plague. The vision of the desert makes Maya conscious of her loneliness. The lizards are bleached into albinos by the desert sun. The rats are also a sort of albinos because they live in the dark and hardly expose themselves to the sun. The rats, the lizards, the snake and the desert all intensify Maya's sense of loneliness and an approaching death. She cries out in agony: "The desert is waiting, the rats and the lizards. They will claim the flesh, the winds will carry the bones away. Mind the wind, shut the windows. Hide, hide." (127-28)

As storm approaches, Maya turns restless. The description of the cloud is lively and metaphorical:

> In the east the sun glared, one eye glared, so white, so hot, that before its gaze each object, dead or alive, cringed: the white bones on the desert shrank, split and crumbled, and in the jungles, green leaves curled, withered, had died. In the west hung dust clouds, sulphur-yellow, iodine tinged, heavy, gloomy, loaded with the respite that comes before storm, violence, murder. (181)

The storm comes at last after a long waiting. The servants run shouting through the rooms. They are wildly excited and run here and there to see whether the doors and windows are locked. Maya feels like a dancer who, waiting to go on stage, "pounds the earth with uncontrollable feet once the hypnotic drumming begins." (187) She experiences an agony in ecstasy, a "pain in magnificence." Nature becomes violent, becomes "red in tooth and claw" and tells upon the spirit of the protagonist, Maya. She experiences a similar storm inside her: "Here was a turmoil a wild chiaroscuro of oven hot colours that churned over and over in a heat swelled bubble around me. It revolved around *me*, about *me*, it was *mine, mine,* this was *mine*." (188)

The rush and whirl outside provide Maya with the feeling of being lifted off the earth into the sunset, as if released from bondage, fate, death and dreariness and from unwanted dreams and liberty. She runs from room to room laughing, Then the storm abates. The wind drops and the evening comes. It is a strange evening as the atmosphere is still, the wind has dropped, "tired of storming" and Maya's thought of Arjuna, her long lost brother brings a faint touch of nostalgia to the evening air.

While the storm reveals the violent and malignant aspect of Nature and its impact on the spirit of the protagonist corresponding to a similar storm inside her shattering the balance of her mind, the cry of the peacocks has an element of pathos in it which sharpens Maya's sense of loneliness, separation and death. The death cry of the peacocks is "blood-chilling." Their shrieks of pain "Pia-Pia—Lover, lover, Mio, mio—I die, I die" is a cry of agony in the force of approaching death. They fight before they mate. Their dance is a dance of liberation like the dance of lord Shiva. Thus "living, they are aware of death. Dying they are in love with life." (95-96) Their cry reminds Maya of her Death-in-life existence: "I heard their cry and echoed it. I felt their thirst as they gazed at the rain clouds, their passion as they hunted for their mates, with them I trembled and panted and paced the burning rocks." (96)

She is carried back to her childhood through memory, to the wild tracks of land which remain eruptions of rock and wilderness to her. She remembers the majestic peacock, trailing over a bronze boulder its "long, burdensome" tail glittering and gleaming in a "thousand shades of carbon blue and green and lamp black." Through the death cry of the peacock, Maya hears the call of the albino astrologer. She identifies herself with the peacocks: "Now that I understood their call, I wept for them, and wept for myself, knowing their words to be mine." (97)

The decisive year has come. Maya does not know whether it is she or Gautama, who is to die the fated death. She spends sleepless nights in the moonlight, that "bland white eye that watched and waited." Gautama and Maya walk up the stairs to the terrace. Maya feels Gautama's words lost to her in the presence of the moon's vast, pure surface which looks like a "great multifoliate rose, waxen white, virginal, chaste and absolute white, holy in its purity, a suffusing glow of its chastity, casting its reflection upon the night with a vast, tender, mother love." (208) Gautama's figure seems to her a "crooked grey shadow" that "transgressed its sorrowing chastity" and she pushes him down to the very bottom.

In *Where Shall We Go This Summer?*, Sita's desire not to give birth to her fifth child is in itself a transgression of Nature. She is afraid of the bloodshed and violence that go with the process of creation. She stands all day on the balcony keeping away the crows that attack a wounded eagle on the roof-top of a neighbouring house, "who winced dreadfully every time she heard a child cry." In that city of flats and "alleys" crows form a shadow civilization. The crows hop clownishly about the rock, on which the sea breaks "scrambling to catch a rotten fish or scraps of edible flotsam left by the waves to stink in the sun." (38) They also sit outside on the ledges and balcony rails of the flats, waiting for the lazy cooks to throw out the kitchen garbage into the alley. They catch them in the mid-air. These "tatterdemalions" are experts in all evil practices that go on in the civilized society like murder, infanticide, incest, theft and robbery, everything is "much practised by these rough, raucous, rasping tatterdemalions." (38) They whistle in ecstasy and wave their wings as they find a wounded or a baby eagle. They laugh and rasp as they whip it with their "bluebottle wings" and tear into it with their "scimitar beaks." The eagle tries to crawl into the shelter of the wall's shadow and its "leaf red" wings scrape the concrete and then its "Gold-beaked" head falls to one side. Sita shouts for a stick and stones. But the crows are indifferent. They are used to a certain amount of opposition and aggression from the human population of the city; "they could tackle it, ignore it, choking with laughter." (39)

Sita watches disbelievingly at Menaka when she crumbles a sheaf of new buds on the small potted plant that Sita had grown on the balcony with much labour. Menaka had painted a monsoon scene by using a number of colours and had given an "authentic rendering of rain." Sita looks at the painting admiringly and then finds Menaka tearing it into pieces because she thinks "they are not worth keeping." All these acts of violence lead Sita to think that "destruction may be the true element in which life survives, and creation merely a freak, temporary, and doomed event." (56) Sita leaves the island and goes with Raman to the mainland, to the city which seems to her a place of solidity and security, "the solidity of streets and the security of houses." But she is disappointed with life in the city, a crust of dull tedium, and she decides to turn back once again to the island, where she would hold her baby safely unborn by magic. The sea would wash the frenzy out of her life: "Perhaps the tides would lull the children too, into smoother, softer beings. The grove of trees would shade them and protect them." (101)

But in the island Sita finds the opposites happen. The children do not enjoy the island. There is always the 'roar' and 'sigh' of the tide. The children are scared of the moaning sound of the casuarinas in the grove, the clattering of the palm leaves hanging over the roof making chinks through which the rain spouts down on to the roof. She finds them "staring at her, watching her as though waiting for her to breakdown and admit failure." (103) It seems to Sita as if to her children, life in the city on Napean Sea Road is "right and proper" and this so-called "escape" to the island is madness. Sita does not find the island any more romantic or magical. If it had any magic in the past it is now buried beneath the "soft grey-green mildew of the monsoon, chilled and choked by it." (103) Sita finds her children moving round and round the ruined house in rain and "whenever their paths crossed every half hour or so, they accused her in silence and she pleaded with them in silence too." (103)

Nature does not remain benign, pleasant and jocund for Sita in the island. It repeatedly reminds her of the futility of her existence and her vain attempts to forget the grim realities of life. The monsoon in the island continues like an "unceasing burial," she finds the children getting bored in the island. Menaka is eager to join the medical college. Karan does not find any game to play in the island. Sita realizes that by escaping to the island, she cannot escape life. The children are excited and delighted at the news of their father's arrival. This leads Sita to think of her children as being disloyal to her, disloyal to the island and its wild nature. She feels ashamed of herself. When Raman comes, Sita has a heated discussion with him. When Raman finally decides to go out of the island Sita feels herself free and released, like the free sea-bird at evening which "wheeled around and began to circle about and then dropped lower and lower towards her home." (150) She follows the footprints of Raman. She sees on the sand a chain of footprints, one following another precisely, logically. Then together they walk up the stone steps to the grove. Standing on the step, Sita sees the rope dangling from the old figtree which the young Moses had tied in the long past when she was a child. She realizes that the island belongs only to her father. It does not belong to her. On the eve of her leaving the island the inhabitants remember her father: "Let her go, who cares? We will only remember him, the father. How he lived, and his magic. The island is his, it is really his." (157)

The barren rocks and hills of Carignano in *Fire on the Mountain* become the projection of Nanda Kaul's self. She is herself lonely, has kept herself aloof from relatives and the society to spend a life of seclusion in the quiet house at Kasauli. The barren landscape, the lonely pine tree, the rocks and hills of Carignano do not provide her the absolute tranquillity of her dreams. It is Raka's intrusion on the one hand and the consciousness of the grim realities of life on the other that come on her way.

The screams of the hoopoes are shrill and maddening. Nanda Kaul rushes to pick up a bright apricot which falls down from the tree and is squashed by its fall. Suddenly she finds a bright hoopoe coming down and tearing at its bright flesh and flying off with a lump in its beak. The sight "did not fill her with delight." (4)

The house at Carignano has a history of violence, murder and death. Nanda Kaul had come here with the desire to enjoy the "stillness and calm" but the letter from her daughter Asha perturbs. She leans over the wooden railing at the back of the house where the yellow rose creeper had blossomed "so youthfully" last month but now reduced to an "exhausted mass of grey creaks and groans" again. Her desire for privacy and freedom, which she could never get as the Vice-Chancellor's wife and for which she has come to the hill side is suggested through the image of the eagle:

> An eagle swept over it, far below her, a thousand feet below, its wings out—spread, gliding on currents of air without once moving its great muscular wings which remained in repose, in control. She had wished, it occurred to her, to imitate that eagle—gliding, with eyes closed. (19)

She watches a lapwing in the mustard fields beyond the garden hedge, "its unven flapping flight through the funeral moonlight." The cries of the nervous bird sharpen her sense of loneliness: "Herself a grey cat, a night prowler, she watched it till it disappeared in that direction of the river, its cries growing fainter. Then rubbing her foot in the grass, she relished the sensation of being alone again." (26)

The garden in the Vice-Chancellor's quarters that was full of trees, "full of too many marauding parrots and squirrels and also too many children who "raided them for fruit" is an extended metaphor of the busy and hectic life of Nanda Kaul among children, relatives and guests. In contrast, the garden of Carignano is an image of bareness and emptiness. She does not want any addition to the garden, which like herself has arrived at a state of "elegant perfection," through a process of age, withering away and elimination. She also does not want to add anything to her own "pared, reduced and radiantly single life." When Raka comes she explores the hills and rocks of Kasauli and gets merged with them for hours together. Like Nanda, Raka wants only one thing: "to be left alone and pursue her own secret life amongst the rocks and pines of Kasauli." (48) She has all the "jealous, guarded instinct" of an explorer.

The destructive aspect of Nature is suggested by images of violence and destruction. The Pasteur institute is an image of violence where the doctors make serum for injections for dog bites. They kill the mad dogs and use them for tests. They throw the bones and ashes of dead animals into the ravine and jackals come at night to that place to chew the bones. The "forest fire" is a threat to the quiet and undisturbed lives of the people of the hill side. Nanda Kaul tells Raka that a whole village may burn in a fire that big. Raka hears the cries of animals and birds burning in that fire. The next morning she finds "a cindery smell" and a layer of ashes that is deposited on Kasauli like a "grey pelt."

The group of langurs with their destructive habits attract Raka. She runs towards them with Ram Lal yelling and waving her arms as they tear leaves off the apricot trees in search of fruit, pluck the flowers and destroy them, dash into the kitchen and grab at potatoes, "baring their teeth and gibbering at whoever came in the way." The sight of destruction fascinates her. The single house on the hills and another unbuilt one attract her like a "strong sea current." There is something "illegitimate, uncompromising and lawless that made her tingle. The scene of devastation and failure somehow drew her, inspired her."

Through the image of prey and predator Desai depicts the violence in Nature. The hoopoe catching the 'moths' in the mid-air and ragging worms out of earth and fighting with the bul-buls are a few instances of such images:

> Closer to closer, the hoopoe promenaded under the apricot trees, smartly and unfurling the striped fan on top of its head. Its young had flown and it appeared to be celebrating, even flouting its independence, its new youth and freedom. It pounced upon grasshopper and stabbed it to death with its victorious beak. (103-4)

When Ila Das telephones Nanda and informs her of her arrival in Carignano, Nanda Kaul becomes distracted for some time. She babbles on the telephone and Nanda turns her head the other way in an effort to escape but she finds a white hen dragging out a worm "inch by resisting inch" from the ground till it "snapped in two." Nanda feels herself like the worm. The violence in the animal world is slowly transferred to the human world. The boys tease Ila Das like langurs. They swing about her long arm and hoot at her little grey top knot and wobble on top of her head, "whooping and hooting, munching and mooing, they ran to the right and left of her, suddenly swerving to bump into her small, brittle person, to send her crocheted and moth-eaten shoulder bag flying or her umbrella spinning." (108)

These acts of violence at last culminate in the rape and tragic death of Ila Das by Preet Singh and his gang. In the evening when Ila Das comes through the forest path, Preet Singh behaves roughly with her. The figure of Preet Singh emerging from the rocks is a ghastly sight in the still quiet hillside:

> Just then a black shape detached itself from the jagged pile of the rock, that last rock between her and the hamlet, and sprang soundlessly at her, She staggered under its weight with a gasp that ripped through her chest. It had her by the throat. She struggled, choking, trying to stretch and stretch and stretch that gasp till it becomes a shout, a shout that the villagers would hear, the red dog would hear, a shout for help. (142)

But nobody comes to her help. The fingers of Preet Singh tighten and Ila Das lies dead, "crushed back, crushed down into the earth, she lay raped, broken, still and finished." (143)

The news of the tragic death of Ila Das shatters Nanda Kaul's world of reverie into pieces. The illusory world which she had created as an emotional shelter completely breaks down: "She had dropped the telephone. With her head still thrown back, she gasped: "No, no it is all a lie! No it cannot be. It was a lie—Ila was not trapped, not dead. She had lied to Raka, lied about everything." (145)

She realizes that all the "graces and glories" with which she has tried to captivate Raka are only a fabrication, tranquillizer pills, which helped her to sleep at night. Nanda Kaul's attempt to escape reality like Sita's escape to Manori in *Where Shall We Go This Summer?* is an exercise in self-deception. Complete involvement in "undiluted reality" represented by Ila Das or "undiluted illusion" like that of Nanda Kaul, both eventually spell tragedy. (M. Prasad, *Anita Desai*, 102)

The fire that Raka sets to the forest is expressive of her resolve to destroy Nanda Kaul's world of make-believe. It is not merely an act of violence as Francine E. Krishna says, but also "an act of purification as if she might burn away the lies and deceit of Nanda's portrayal of her childhood as well as the violence of her own." (*Indian Literature,* 169)

There is always an interaction between the human and the non-human world as much of the imagery in this novel deal with the animate non-human features of Nature and the landscape like animals, birds and insects. These images are not static rather they change according to the change within the characters. For example when Raka is strolling with Nanda Kaul and happens to see the langurs they seem to her funny creatures but after the traumatic experience in the club with people under masks resembling langurs when she meets the langurs for the second time they seem to her like pierrots, clowns and bandits.

The animals and birds which are described in connection with Nanda are benign like domestic hens, house flies or the animals of her imaginary world such as the Himalayan bear, crocodile or leopard. But Raka is described as a wild animal, "as secretive as a little wild bird, or an insect that hides." She is also compared to a jackal: "Raka no more needed or wanted a house than a jackal did or a cicade. She was a wild creature—wild, wild, wild, thought Nanda Kaul." (103) Violence emerging out of the human world preys upon all the three major characters of this novel. Nanda Kaul is a victim of the violence of indifference of her husband. Ila Das is a victim of rape and murder. Raka is a victim of the world of her parents that she is born to. All the violence of the human world correspond to the violence in Nature that are expressed through the images of the hoopoes, the hen dragging out the worm, the destructive monkies, snakes, night jars and jackals. Everything is engulfed by the forest fire at the end suggesting the "funeral fire," the fire of purgation:

> Lately her great-grandmother had bored her with it, played it with such theatrical ardour as to make it as unreal as theatre. It made her ache for the empty house on the charred hill, the empty summer-stricken view of the snakes, bones and smoking kilns—all silent, and a forest fire to wipe it all away, leaving ashes and silence. (120)

The same image of birds and insects is also significant in *Clear Light of Day*. Tara finds no change in the garden of her parents's house. The gardener has planted jasmines in the garden and has watered the plants. Flocks of green parrots come to the garden shrieking and settle on the sunflowers and "rip their black-seeded centres to bits" while mynahs hop up and down on the lawn "quarrelling over insects" and Bim's cat gets annoyed when the mynahs's shriek. The scent from the flower garden, a "scent of spider lilies" resembles the fragrance of "ladies newly bathed, powdered and scented" for the evening. The uncared for and teeming gardens outside resemble the lack of orderliness in the lives of the neighbours: "On either side of their garden were more gardens neighbours' houses, as still and faded and shabby as theirs, the gardens as over-grown and neglected and teeming with wild, uncontrolled life." (23-24)

The garden, though a symbol of pattern and order, also turns malevolent sometimes. The experience of Bim and Tara in the Lodi garden is an ironical reminder of this. The experience is symbolic of the sacrificial life of Bim. It also reveals the escapist in Tara. Tara and Bim visit the Lodi garden with the Mishra family in the spring time. While strolling in the garden, Tara descends down the grassy slope and sees Bim still standing at the top, attacked by a swarm of bees. She is in their midst as if she is their "chosen queen made prisoner": "It was a bee's festival, a celebration, Bim their appointed victim, the sacrificial victim on whom they had dropped the ceremonial shawl drawing it close about her neck as she stood dropping, shivering under the weight of their guazy wings, their blue-black humming." (135) When Bim is attacked by the bees, Tara escapes from that place frenziedly running to the Mishras for help. She is scolded by Raja for her escapist nature as she leaves Bim alone and helpless.

The thirst of summer, the parched and barren atmosphere of summer correspond to the dry and parched existence of the protagonist Deven in *In Custody*. When Deven returns to Delhi, he stands near the doorway and sees the sparrows nesting in the skylight twitter and quarrel, scattering twigs as they rustle about their nests, somebody outside shouting Su-ra-hi keeping the earthen jars on the back of his donkey. The coming of the devastating summer announced by the Surahi hawker outside is already a felt experience for Deven: "The call that had seemed to announce summer, heat and thirst—but summer was already here, devastating everything, laying waste his life, like this desolate room." (170)

There are references to "temperature," "heat," "thirst" and summer throughout the novel which are suggestive of the "parched" dry life of the protagonist Deven:

> The temperature that day was a hundred and fourteen degrees. The neem trees along the street dropped stricken, encased in dust. The horses between the shafts of the old tonga stood with their legs sloping under them, their necks swaying between their knees. Even the flies that adhered to their muzzles and flanks had ceased to buzz and crawl and appeared to be stuck on with glee. (190-91)

Deven enters a park and sits on an empty bench. He sees the dome and the eastern wall of the mosque. The sun is very bright, almost dazzling his eyes. The enormous arched doorway that soars upwards to the dome looks like a vast bubble. It looks absolutely still, silent as if it is the silent answer to his questioning: "Since it was silent, he could not hear it, but he felt it impress its shape upon his eyelids, very gently, very lightly, and like fingertips pressing them down to sleep." (192)

But the summer with its dryness, its heat and thirst is not going to continue for ever. When the heat becomes unbearable for Deven, he hears thunders in the distance, perhaps, announcing that the monsoon is drawing closer. Deven thinks it has come because he cannot endure the heat and waiting anymore.

When Deven receives the letter from Nur, he realizes that the relationship between them, between art and the artist is still inextricable in spite of occasional misunderstanding. Deven has a vision of Nur's bier, heaped with flowers and women in the family crying and wailing around. He hears the funeral music. He imagines that when Nur's body would be placed inside the grave, he would be in charge of the widows and his son. Deven looks at the whirlpool in the water. Nature takes a different colour with the change of outlook of the protagonist. The sky is gradually filled with a grey light. It is no longer dark. The grey light slowly dissolves the "dense blackness" of the night. It "glistened" upon a field of white pampass grass which wave in the slow breeze. Deven feels that he has already become the custodian of Nur's very soul and spirit by accepting his poetry, which he cannot abandon under any pressure. The novel ends on an optimistic note: "soon the sun would be up and blazing." (204) The possibility of brightness, freshness and regeneration suggested by the sunlight, is also indicative of a possible change in the present condition of the protagonist.

In her latest novel *Baumgartner's Bombay*, the different aspects of Nature are so influenced by the life in the city that they lose their inherent charm and turn insipid, blank and colourless like the lives of the characters. As Lotte observes out of her window: "Right at the top, a layer of sky. A blank sky, as always with neither colour, nor form. Empty, after noon light. Daylight, perpetual light and blankness." (4)

Life in a busy metropolis like Bombay is always on the go, always brisk. People seldom find time to look at Nature during day time. It is also due to the hot sun and the busy life of the day that they come to the sea shore in the evening to spend sometime away from the hurly burly city life: "Baumgartner did not turn towards the sea. That was for the evening, when the breeze came up with the tide, and the sun fell headlong into the waves, livid and melodramatic in its orange and purple flames and people strolled, for pleasure buying themselves peanuts to eat or coconut to drink from, and one was not conspicuous if one loitered too." (8) But for the protagonist Baumgartner, Nature loses all charm when he finds her mother playing a duet with the young Friedmann: "She smiled at Hugo when he came in but did not stop playing." (41)

Nature becomes a metaphor of indifference; his mother's indifference to his father and his family. Instead of acting as a benign shaping spirit the garden turns out for Hugo to be a disturbing presence. Being too small though he could not discover a meaning in his mother's indifference but surely he felt something for which he did not like to stay in that place for long.

The human world always interacts with the world of nature in the novels of Anita Desai. Nature in her novels acts both as a consoling agent and also as a disturbing presence. It provides solace to the characters by taking them away from the world of pain and suffering and at the same time makes them conscious of the grim existential realities. There is a constant interaction between the inner world of the protagonist and the outer world of nature and in the process of this interaction, an intense vision of the ambivalence of life is projected. In the novels of Anita Desai, Nature thus appears as an ironic presence that pervades life in terms of both its materiality and spirituality.

The Rites of Childhood: Memory and Innocence

> Yes, now that I go over it in my mind, my childhood was one in which much was excluded, which grew steadily more restricted, unnatural even, and in which I lived as a toy princess in a toy world. But it was a pretty one. (*Cry, the Peacock*, 89)

The desire to capture and hold the "toy world" of "blood red ruby" (94) and "painted butterfly" (94) haunts the characters of Desai's novels. There is a growing incompatibility between the world in which the characters are brought up and the world thrust upon them by circumstances as they grow. Most of Desai's characters are orphans or either of their parents is dead. For example, Maya and Sita are motherless. The mother of Tara, Bim, Raja and Baba die when they are very small. Monisha, Nirode and Amla are both physically and psychologically estranged from their mother, and their father dies when they are still children. The joy and trauma of their childhood experiences get reflected in the attitudes and sensibilities of all these characters. The obsession with dream and memory and the urge to escape the dreadful reality of social existence lead the characters to an introspective stance. They turn to the innocent days of the past, the pleasure and joy of childhood. This nostalgic sense of innocence leads to a schizophrenic tendency in Maya, Sita and Monisha whereas for Tara, Amla and Sarala, it brings frustration and despair.

Maya speaks of her childhood as "my happiest days." The excessive love of her father made her a wayward and high-strung child. She recollects her father's soothing words which were like "a stream of cold water that tumbled through the ferns of Darjeeling or like the cold pern mists that crept over the blue hills and poured into the valley." (8) The toy world of her childhood painted in her "favourite tunes" is a world of the "velvet bugs," and the "blood red ruby." Maya's memory of her childhood is articulated in terms of the images of intense sensuousness. The breakfast she used to have with her father as a child was almost like "a revel of elves and fairies who feast on melons and syrups by moonlight." (43) In her childhood, she was almost like a princess:

> As a child, I enjoyed, princess like, a sumptuous fare of the fantasies of the Arabian Nights, the glories and bravado of Indian mythology long and astounding tales of princes and regal queens, jackals and tigers and being my father's daughter, of the lovely English and Irish fairy tales as well, that were read out to me by him. (43)

Maya remembers the spring when she was at Lucknow with her father. She strolls among the vegetables in the garden with her father. She feels "ecstatic" amidst the flowers, the butterflies and the blue sky. When her eyes get tired of the sun and brightness, she rolls over her stomach and kicks up her legs and gazes into the "serene green of the grass; lush enough to graze in, drown in." (36) She closes her eyes and listens to the ecstatic music of the insects. The atmosphere is charged with the vibrant music of the grasshopper like a "violent string set into motion." Maya falls into a reverie as she opens her eyes to find the "velvet bugs" in the lawn.

In contrast, in Gautama's family "one did not speak of love, far less of affection." (46) Her marriage to Gautama is not out of love but is based on her father's choice. Apart from the temperamental difference between Gautama and Maya, there is a wide difference in age too. Her husband's indifference intensifies her loneliness in the house. She cries out in agony, "yes, it is his hardness—no, no, not hardness but the distance he coldly keeps from me." (40) The nerve-racking experience of being ignored by Gautama and his family impels her to recoil to her childhood days. The memory of the albino astrologer disturbs her. She remembers the warning of the astrologer when she was still a small child: "Four years after your marriage, so the stars prophesy, and the space between your eyes, the mark there, supports this prophesy." (37)

This memory of the astrologer, stirred by the death of the dog Toto deepens her obsession with death. Several other things like the death-cry of the peacocks, Mrs. Lal's child that enters the room during the party create a sense of futility in her. She visits the cabaret with her husband but there she is reminded of the bear-dance that she had seen in her childhood: "I gaze at this magnificent beast from whose thick coat the gloss has sunk into dust, from whose tenebrous eyes all pride and power have gone, leaving only an intent determination to remain tearless." (87) Maya perceives a strange similarity of her own present predicament with that of the beast of her memory.

Gautama considers Maya's regressive tendency as rooted in a "father fixation." He considers her father responsible for making her a spoilt baby, a neurotic: "Neurotic that's what you are. A spoilt baby, so spoilt she can't bear one adverse word. Everyone must bring a present for little Maya that is what her father taught her." (115) Gautama considers her father responsible for making her believe that all that is important in the world is "to possess—possess—riches, comforts, posies, dollies, loyal retainers—all the luxuries of the fairy tales you were brought up on. Life is a fairy tale to you still." (115) Her father brought her up in the "picture book fashion." Maya, in Gautama's estimation, knows nothing about realities and common human existence. She leads a life of delusion. She still walks on the memory garden of childhood and dreams about the fairies who sleep on buds and considers Gautama as the "wicked bogeyman who refuses to play" along with her, who cuts down all the pretty posies with a lash of his whip. Maya thinks of herself as different from Gautama and his family: "I am different from all of you." (117) But Gautama misunderstands the meaning of "different." He thinks: "if one must have a real, solid, personal world, why not create one within oneself, to detach one self into when the world around grows either too boring or too hectic." (117)

A letter from her long-lost brother Arjuna again stirs her memory. Arjuna is a peculiar child. Unlike Maya, he never likes the garden and the flowers. He has no interest in their father's world of parties, revels and drinks. Unlike Maya, Arjuna is a rebel from his very childhood. Maya also remembers Neila, who had married a man suffering from tuberculosis. All these memories of the past and the inability to adjust herself to an indifferent family make her feel utterly lonely and desolate. When a child, her father used to fulfil all her demands. Every summer he used to ask her to suggest the name of the place which she would like to visit. But after marriage when Maya tells Gautama about her desire to go to the South to see the Kathakali dance, he irreverently dismisses the idea. Gautama's mother is hardly concerned with Maya's health and she pays no attention to her. She only asks her, "when will your father send me another cheque Maya? Tell him I need it urgently—the nurses in the creche have not been paid this month." (47-48)

Maya completely withdraws herself from the rest of the family and passes her days in utter loneliness. She gradually loses the balance of her mind. The "dust storm" outside corresponds to a storm inside her and she cries out in agony: "Ah storm, storm, wonderful, infidel storm, blow, blow! I cried, and ran on and on, from room to room laughing as maniacs laugh once the world gives them up and surrenders them to their freedom." (190) Gautama thinks it very unnatural and considers it as mere father fixation. He thinks that perhaps because of this Maya agreed to marry him, a man so much older than herself.

After the death of Gautama, Maya is completely absorbed in her childhood memories. Her anguish accentuates at the decay of the world of rubies and butterflies: "when I lay in bed at last, I continued to think of them, uneasily, restlessly, connecting them with a dream I had once had as a child, with the convoluted history behind a ruby red as blood, with the brief life of a painted butterfly." (94) She makes futile attempts to capture and hold it but in vain. She loses the balance of her mind and returns to her infantile state, into a second childhood. She starts playing with dolls, laughs like a child, falls upon the picture books and opens the drawers. Nila and her mother hear "the patter of a child's laughter cascading up and down the scales of some new delight, a brilliant peacock's feather perhaps? Then it stopped, suddenly, and they heard a different voice calling, shrilly, and desperately, from some unimaginable realm of horror calling out in great dread." (217-18) Maya's fond nostalgia for childhood thus culminates in an almost hysterical longing for the splendid delight of a child and the tragic awareness of the impossibility of its realization.

Nirode in *Voices in the City* is unable to shake himself off the clutches of his past. He does not deliberately seek the past but the past nevertheless holds on to him. He wants to forget his past for two reasons; it reminds him of his failures, and it develops a mother-obsession in him as he is reminded of his mother's illicit relationship with Major Chadha. When he reads a letter from his mother he feels like "sinking his teeth through a sweet mulberry to bite into a caterpillar's entrails." (37) Nirode's memory of his childhood is a mixture of sweet and bitter feelings. He recalls his childhood with bitterness as he compares himself with his brother Arun, who is a bright student, while Nirode is a "congenital failure." He knows that this is the reason why his father showers money on Arun's higher education. The brothers and sisters acknowledge Arun's talents. Nirode is an "emotional and disorderly school boy" who falls down from the horse and declares to his father that he hates horses and sports. He writes verses on exercise books which are "confiscated and scrawled over with the obscenities of his happier colleagues in school." (7) A sense of inferiority consumes him throughout his life and he moves from failure of failure. As a child, Nirode feels that the love and affection of his parents is less for him than for Arun and this feeling of inadequacy impedes the full blooming of his personality. He feels like "a long weed undulating under water, a weed that could live only in aqueous gloom, would never rise and sprout into clear day-light." (63)

The sweet memory of his childhood delights him when he remembers his mother playing chinese checkers with her children sitting on the bright mats. She puts them to sleep by telling stories from the *Maha-*

bharata. But the sweet memory of his mother's affection blends with an intense hatred for her when the figure of Major Chadha appears before him: "How helpful was this Chadha, providing her with male company and admiration. How solidly he planted himself on her little square chair, gay with Tibetan tapestries, how he cleared his throat before she began to chatter herself, with ravishing gaiety and youthfulness." (37)

Amla tells Dharma that her mother is a sophisticated and refined lady, whereas her father is a drunkard and is not interested in the finer things of life. The children are therefore more drawn to their mother than to their father. She is a source of consolation and courage to them. When the children grow up, their mother is separated from them and stays in Kalimpong. She writes long, warm letters to her children. But her letters infuriate Nirode. Something seems to have gone wrong somewhere in the relationship between the mother and her children. Because of this Nirode feels as if a barbed wire fence stands between him and his mother. Nirode can still hear the sound of the footsteps and the voice of Major Chadha who with his "bestial jaws and small eyes and hairy hands repelled Nirode" (27-28) and can see his mother sitting with Major Chadha "smiling a slow sensual smile." (28) His mother's relation with Chadha disturbs Nirode even in his dreams and he mutters in sleep: "No mother, you can't." (26) Nirode's mother-complex, sense of inferiority and failure make him "a misfit hero," (1971:202) "a rootless nihilist" (Irma Maini, 1977:222) and a "psychic outlaw." (222) He turns a rebel and starts disliking the entire world that could offer him no crusade, no pilgrimage.

Amla remembers the long summer holidays of her childhood playing with the gardener's children and going off to the orchard to build camps and fuss over dolls. She tells Dharma about her father who meets an automobile accident and dies: "It seems to me that was the one active violent moment of his life, that the rest of it he spent in sleeping and drinking and idling." (207) She also remembers her brother Arun telling her that father taught him to play cricket. Their father drinks and smiles a "spiteful smile." She remembers her mother crying but Amla does not understand the reason of it as father behaves very politely with the children. Amla recollects her mother as the most beautiful woman she knows and very accomplished like "a well cut jewel." She says that she has inherited the high cheekbones of her mother who is the daughter of a Nepalese woman. Unlike Nirode, Amla's recollection of her mother is full of appreciation and admiration.

Sitting in the night club, Jit remembers the "lost world of his childhood." The orchestra, the busy waiters, the dancers—amidst all these Jit continues to mourn the "lost world that he seemed to have rediscovered at the bottom of his glass of beer." (103) Jit recollects his past sitting in the garden in the evening. He tells Nirode: "I like to think of my father, it consoles me to think of him sitting in the garden in the evening." (103) Under the promegranate tree, Jit's father would split one fruit open with his hand and show the children the globules laid side by side in "perfect design" inside the fruit and they would eat them with pepper and salt. His mother collects blood red flowers and offers them in her prayer. Jit wonders how his wife Sarala laughs at his suggestion to make space for prayer in their house.

Sita, the sensitive protagonist of *Where Shall We Go This Summer?* undergoes acute mental agonies and escapes into the island of Manori to achieve the miracle of not giving birth to her fifth child. She returns to the island with an obsessive desire to capture the purity and innocence of her childhood. She wants to recapture the pristine world of her childhood both for herself and for the child.

Sita's father presides over the island like a magician. Sita sees the island as a "piece of magic, a magic mirror." In that paradise of her father, "Moses and Miriam are the original inhabitants." (61) The natives of the island believe that her father could cure scorpion bites, could change the taste of the water. Kantiamma says, "he knew magic." Like Maya, Sita is also motherless from her childhood. Jiban tells her the story of her mother who ran away to Benares, which she does not believe. "You needn't believe me if you don't want to. But I have heard people talk about it. Of course he added . . . she may be dead by now." (84) Sita cannot believe the idea of a mother alive and staying at Benares away from her children. She has never felt the absence of a mother because she has been born and brought up amidst a crowd: "Sita had imagined she came into the world motherless—and the world was crowded enough so." (84)

Sita has an unusual childhood, "full of large meaningful happenings, but also as very trivial, "full of disappointments. It comes as a tremendous depression to her." (Jain, *Stairs to the Attic*, 11) She has never lived the life of "ruby and pearl" though she has seen, the "rubies and pearls crushed in the mortar." (85) She does not remember ever wanting or waiting for her mother but she finds herself turning into a wanderer always searching after the ghost: "who, what was she?" (85) She tries to sketch an imaginary mother in her mind. She feels like asking about her mother to her father and her step-sister Rekha but she cannot as "there was no intimacy between her and Rekha that would permit such a question." (86)

As a child Sita has sensed an illicit relationship between her father and Phoolmaya and also an incestuous relationship between her step-sister Rekha and her father. She ponders about the real nature of her father and the cause of her mother deserting her children. As a child Sita never belongs to a single family but to the whole society: "She belonged, if to anyone to this whole society that existed at this particular point in history like a lamb does to its folk and saw no reason why she should belong to one family alone." (85)

For the second time when Sita visits the island, it is an escape and a release from the city life. After twenty years the island has substantially changed. She misses the milieu of innocence and purity of her childhood. Her children Menaka and Karan, both fail to adjust to the primitive life of the island. She realizes, "Life must be continued and all its business." (101) The island, the "protective chrysalis of childhood" (M. Prasad, 72) finally disappoints her. She gets disappointed with the islanders as much as the islanders get disappointed with her. In the end the same people who sing the praises of her father condemn Sita.

Nostalgia for lost innocence and the awareness of a decaying life are the recurrent themes in Anita Desai. In *Fire on the Mountain* the contrast between the two is evident in the two characters, Raka and Nanda Kaul. Raka's love for loneliness is natural. She is "a recluse by nature, by instinct." She was "born to it simply" (48) whereas in Nanda Kaul, this is deliberate as a "vengeance for a long life of duty and obligation." (48) The spontaneous detachment and withdrawal in case of Raka is the outcome of a tortured childhood, the traumatic experience she has had as a child, which still comes to her in dream or like a vision. Her father returns home from a party "stumbling and crashing through the curtains of night." (71) He abuses her mother in filthy language and beats her up which makes Raka cover under her bed clothes. She wets the mattress in fright. As the stream of urine passes through her legs, she feels like a stream of blood passing down her leg. Her mother lies down on the floor and closes her eyes and weeps. In the darkness, under her flat Raka feels: "the wet jelly of her mother's being squelching and quivering so that she didn't know where to put her feet and wept as she tried to get free of it. Ahead of her, no longer on the ground but the same distance now, her mother was crying. Then it was a jackal crying." (71-72) These experiences have made Raka a peculiar child. She is unlike other children. She never demands anything or expects anything. Her peculiarity surprises Nanda Kaul. Raka has become a withdrawn child who is very different from Nanda's own children or grand-children. Like her grandmother, Raka wants only one thing—"to be left alone and pursue her own secret life amongst the rocks and pines of Kasauli." (48)

The lack of communication between Raka and Nanda Kaul suggests, as R.S. Sharma observes, a "sickness of soul" imposed upon them from outside. Nanda Kaul lives a kind of life which does not involve her "self." It is full on the surface but empty at the core. The trauma of childhood, on the other hand, "had blunted the native thrust of Raka's soul." Thus they both "seek to exclude what they need most—the security and fulfilment of love." (*Littcrit*, 5)

Raka's indifference accentuates Nanda Kaul's desire for tender love. She tries her best to win Raka. She recreates an imaginary childhood, in which she projects some of her own longings as a child. This fantasy world is based on the memory of an adventurous father who brings home the relics and menageries from Tibet. By creating this projected childhood Nanda Kaul herself arrives at a second childhood: "She pouted, childishly, one might have said she had arrived at her second childhood if one believed in such things. She looked so exactly like a baby thwarted, wanting attention she did not get, as she stalked through the hot, waiting house." (101)

The central motif of the novel *Clear Light of Day* is taken from Emily Dickinson's poem "memory is a strange bell—Jubilie and knell." Desai follows a theme that corresponds to Eliot's concept of Time and its effect on human beings:

> See how they vanish,
> The faces and places,
> with the self which
> as it could, loved them,
> To become renewed, transfigured
> in another pattern (4)

When Tara visits her parents's house in Old Delhi after her marriage, she finds no change there. While moving across the lawn, Tara transposes herself to her childhood when she accompanies her mother to the garden. Her mother following the doctor's advice strolls up and down the rose walk. Usually her mother does not take exercise. Either she sits at the card table playing or sleeps on her bed with a suffering face "tilted upward in warning so that Tara did not dare approach." (102) Her mother continues to keep that distance from Tara. Tara remembers:

> Even now she kept her distance. She paced slowly, obediently, her arms folded, her chin sunk into her neck, as if considering a hand of cards, while Tara in her nightie, skipped and danced after her, her bare feet making tracks through the misty dew on the grass. (102)

Now when Tara dances in joy at the sight of a snail. Bim is surprised to see "a grown up woman, mother of grown up daughters, still child enough to play with a snail?" (2) Like a child Tara shouts at the sight of a snail in the garden, "an eternal, miniature Sisyphus." (2) Sitting in the room, Tara feels:

> the boredom of her childhood, her youth were stored here in the room under the warm dusty red rugs in the bloated yellowed photographs in the oval frames, everything, everything that she had so hated as a child and that was still preserved here as if this were the store room of some dull, uninviting provincial museum. (20-21)

She recalls her parents who used to sit there, playing cards with friends. She feels the presence of the very spirit of her parents. The "paper world," the card-games of their parents, causes serious reactions in the children. Raja swears that one day he would leap into the table in a lion mask "brandishing a torch and set fire to this paper world of theirs" (22) and flashing her sewing scissors, Bim declares: "she would creep in secretly at night and snip all the cards into bits." (22) But Tara is different. She simply sucks her finger and retreats down the veranda to Aunt Mira's room and tucks herself up in the plum coloured quilt "that smelt so comfortably of the aged relation" and her little cat lay beside her. She never feels like wrecking their parents's hobby or divert their attention: "it would have frightened her a bit if they had come away, followed her and tried to communicate with her." (22)

Tara's memory of her father giving an injection to her mother revives her suspicion that her father has killed her mother. She is still haunted by the memory of her father entering the room, leaning over her mother's bed and "quickly, smoothly press a little syringe into her mother's arm that lay crookedly on the blue cover." (22) In spite of the attempts of Aunt Mira, Bim and Raja to explain to her what it really was, Tara cannot free herself of the "original stab of suspicion."

But Bim does not seem to have lived Tara's kind of childhood. The very thought of childhood breeds cynicism in her. She tries to forget her childhood. It reminds her of the ingratitude of her family members. She does not want to return to her childhood, even through memory. She questions Tara: "But you would not want to return to life as it used to be, would you?" She hates all that dullness, boredom and waiting for their parents till late night. She thinks no one would secretly or sincerely prefer to return to such a childhood.

Bim remains a spinster all through her life. She works as a lecturer in a local college. Time has changed the sweet relation between Bim and Raja from brother-and-sister to that of a landlord and tenant. The memory of her childhood fills her heart with a sense of loss and rejection. She recollects how on the terrace she had cut Tara's hair which had made Tara cry: "What an uproar there was. And here you are your hair grown long again, and it's mine that's cut chort. Only no one cares when I cut mine." (26)

But Tara as a child always expects to be treated like a princess, like Maya in *Cry, the Peacock*: "perhaps a jewel ring, Tara always expecting to find treasure, to make her fortune, discovers herself a princess." (153) She remains the "baby of the family" until the new baby arrives. The new baby Baba is slow in every respect. All their efforts to make him talk fail. The children are brought up with much care by Aunt Mira. Bim and Raja are closer in age and Tara is the smaller and weaker one, "born to trail behind others." While playing the games of hide and seek in the garden, in the summer evenings Raja is the leader and the two sisters are engaged in "frenzied pursuit, tearing their dresses and bruising their knees" to find Raja and "call him captive."

The students at school consider Tara "unbearably snobbish and conceited." (125) They always single her out and smirk to see her "scolded" and "have her homework flung at her in rage." (125) Bim deliberately avoids her while playing basket-ball with the bigger girls to avoid her "anti-social misery" (125) which she thinks is "contagious." Tara becomes a morose and lonely child. She wanders about the playground alone during lunch break watching the kites that circle in the white sky. The children at school think that she is "too conceited to join them in their songs and their gossip and clatter." (125) She is horrified by the two sensational incidents which happen at school: the killing of the mad dog and the love affair of the new teacher with the Buddhist monk.

Both Tara and Bim are dissatisfied with their childhood. Their parents are indifferent towards the children. They come home late at night. The negligence of the parents creates a vacuum in their heart. Their parents sit playing bridge in the green lit aquarium at the card-room "unaware of their daughter's presence outside, and to whom it had never occurred that the child was now a young girl and might like to be taken out with them." (138) Bim tries to escape from the unpleasantness at home by concentrating on her studies which perhaps she thinks is a way out. By concentrating on her studies, Bim thinks she can avoid the insipid atmosphere at home. The parents's continual absence from home, their disinterest in their children, the silent suffering of their mother are at the root of the silent desperation that pervades the house.

Tara's growing obsession with childhood is a clear indication of thc fact that she thinks time is static. She does not admit the growth of time. She cannot make herself free from the clutches of time past and adjust herself to time present. But gradually she recognizes the significance of the process of time. She advises Bim to attend Moyana's wedding and to forget all about it. But Bim continues to remain "entangled in the dense musty web."

The novel *In Custody* has also patches of memory woven into the narrative. Deven is upset by a visit of his childhood friend Murad. Murad is the "spoilt rich boy" with money in his pocket for cinema and cigarettes and Deven is the "poor widow's son who could be bribed and bought to do anything for him." (11) This basis of their friendship has now changed. Even after getting educated and after becoming a lecturer in a college in Mirpore, Deven remains the same "two-cigarette man" who offers "bread and potato curry" in a small, dirty restaurant to Murad who is a rich and established journalist now. All through his childhood and youth, Deven has learnt "to lie low and remain invisible." As in the childhood, the rich spoilt boy Murad lures him into making money by writing for his magazine.

When Hugo Baumgartner recalls his childhood it is with a mixed feeling of pleasure and pain. He remembers an authoritarian father who walked as if "there was no obstacle and no hesitation" and a loving but over-protective mother whose "soft, sweet-smelling aris" which led him to almost an imprisonment in the flat.

The memory of childhood has a long lasting effect on Baumgartner. He remembers the Sunday when inside a cafe his father had offered him beer and how he climbed on his father's knees and drank the beer which was cold and bitter, smelt of wet straw and tasted of steel. The bitter taste of the beer made him gasp and withdraw, froth moustached to make his father laugh as he never laughed at home." (*Baumgartner's Bombay*, 24)

The innocent experiences of his childhood always ended in a quaver that made Hugo, a peculiar child, lonely and withdrawn. The memory of the hedgehog which he had brought home and took so much care of it that it died due to overfeeding, resulted in despair. The innocence of childhood expresses itself through another experience. When Hugo was asked by his mother to bring a packet of butter from the shop, he remembers how he had dropped the coins on the stairs and how in darkness while coming home, he was so scared that the butter and its wrapper had become one by the time he reached home.

Hugo remembers his first day in school. Like other children he also waited for his mother and when his mother came before she could shame him with 'an embrace' he "snatched the cone out of her hand in jubilation and held it up for others to see." (33) But the children were gone. No one was there to see him. After eating the toffee with his mouthful he blamed his mother for coming late and complained, "you don't look like everyone else's mother. Why don't you look like other mothers?" (33)

Hugo's intense desire to go with his father to see the race course was shattered to pieces when his father refused to take Hugo with him. With the innocence of a child he waited near the door, open mouth, with a hope that his father would open the door and come to take him to the race course. But he was disappointed. The foot steps on the stairs receded and disappeared: "Then Hugo moved with a roar. He ran to the window and beat on the glass as if to break it, so that his mother had to hold him away even if she was kicked and beaten." (34)

The memory of the christmas day is symbolic of Hugo's defeat in victory. It was a day when "triumph had come his way" but "he had not been able to accept." In the christmas party though there were buns, mugs of cocoa and other things, "his eyes, heart and mouth remained fixed on the tree glittering in its finery, the candle flames darting at the shiny surfaces, turning it to a thing of fire and stars fallen out of the sky."

The sense of outlandishness is deeply rooted in Baumgartner from his very childhood but the reasons are not known even to him. This extra-ordinariness of Desai's characters which make them alienated from the outer world and drive them inward was present in Hugo when he was a very small boy. On the christmas day Fraulein called children one by one to accept the gifts. Hugo's name was called last. He was to be given the glass globe. Instead of moving forward to accept the gift, Hugo looked down at his toes. He did not look up. He did not even come to accept the gift. The children pushed him to come up and accept the gift but he did not move till Fraulein handed the gift to the smallest child Elizabeth Kleini. After that Hugo had an experience of shame, that he did not belong to the picture book world, the faery world every child belongs to: "Then the agony was over and he could collapse into the dark ditch of shame. What was the shame? The sense that he didn't belong to the picture book world of the fir trees, the gifts and the celebration? But no one had said that. Was it just that he sensed he did not belong to the radiant, the triumphant of the world? A strange sensation, surely for a child." (36)

Baumgartner has also not forgotten the humiliating jokes of the school mates pointed at his nose, "Baumgartner's dumb, has a nose like a thumb," and has tried to find out the relation between his nose and the thumb, and that he had formed a habit that never left him.

The sense of an incomplete childhood also torments Hugo Baumgartner like Desai's other characters such as Nirode, Raka, Monisha and Sita. When he recollects the remarkable sight of his mother flowering in the company of her friends who she had been in the habit of slipping off to see and visit alone when his father would take Hugo out for a few hours: "Somehow she had not liked them to meet these friends of her girlhood." (45) Baumgartner also remembers how happy his mother looked while recollecting her experience of going straight from school to see Max Reinhardt's production Lohengrin. Her cheeks radiated as she laughed remembering the embarrassing situation there but Hugo at that time was thinking of his father:

> Hugo instead, remembered the figure of his father, left behind in a wrapping of blankets; he felt uneasy, sensing a rift, a break between his parents that might have existed for all these years but of which he was only now really aware. He kept his eye on his mother, suddenly so much younger, and he exposed and vulnerable. (46)

Hugo's mother's interest in poetry, especially in new poets and their work was disturbing him. Hugo was unfamiliar with it all: "He thought that he understood as little as his father did, something they put down to her youth in a university town while they were two masculine city dwellers." (48) The reading of poetry continued for a long time. It might have gone on all night if Hugo had not interrupted. He could not tolerate anymore: "He could not allow his mother to continue with her pretence that she had returned to her youth, that her adulthood could be ignored. Seeing her so childishly irresponsibly blithe, he was driven to an adult decision." (76) Turning around, he saw them listening admiringly to Albert reading a poem about deer by the lake that he called, "The Kaiser of the Woods" and blurted out: "Mama, Komm, we must go back to papa now." For this he was scolded by his mother when they travelled back in a train, coming home when his mother opened the door, she screamed and as they ran towards the kitchen they could smell the odour coming out of it and when the kitchen door burst open they saw "the body sagging out of the open oven door." And when they lifted him, the head "waggled helplessly out of their arms."

After that incident Hugo never went to school as he felt his mother wanted him always by her side. Hugo and his mother remained in the compartment looking after each other with "stricken concern." People in the neighbourhood occasionally visited them with magazines, rolls and jam. The Gentleman from Hamburg installed his name in the shop downstairs. After that, one by one, all their valuable things were removed downstairs by his mother's orders. When Hugo opened his mouth in protest, his mother "laid her finger on her lips and whispered the old saying, "step-children must behave doubly well." Their apartment became strangely empty and this "emptiness matched the silence into which they sank." (51) Then one day the Gentleman from Hamburg, Herpfuchl suggested to send Hugo downstairs to work in the office, his mother readily agreed and that was the beginning of Hugo's "first lesson in the stiffening effect of hardship." (51)

The use of flashback is a recurrent narrative technique with Anita Desai. She asserts that the experiences of childhood are the most "vivid and lasting experiences which have a strong impact on the entire life of a person." She uses the memories of the past as a method of "evaluating the individual's relationship with the present." (J. Jain, 14) This regressive mode acts as a medium of self-knowledge and a strategy for confrontation with reality. It is also an efficacious technique to cover a large area of a tiny territory of human life. As Anita Desai herself spells out the objective of her narrative technique of flashbacks into childhood: "every human being's territory is really very small. And all you can explore is a very tiny section of this territory, and this is a more interesting technique than covering large area." ("Interview," *Stairs to the Attic*, 14)

The Tragic Vision: Defeat and Disillusionment

> All order is gone out of my life, all formality. There is no plan, no peace, nothing to keep me within the patterns of familiar, everyday living and doing that becomes those whom God means to live on earth. (*Cry, the Peacock*, 179)

Life, to Desai is a "snail found, a pearl lost." (*Clear Light of Day*, 103) It is "traceless, meaningless, only a conundrum." (*Voices in the City*, 125) She depicts the futility of existence and man's vain attempts to survive in the face of all "calamities" through an exploration not of the "social" man but of "the lone individual." (Belliappa, 26) Desai's vision of life is one of ambivalence that encompasses defeat and disillusionment as well as acceptance and affirmation. Her fictional world is a world of chaos and confusion. It is an ambivalent world where we find the co-existence of incompatibilities and contradiction such as involvement and indifference, emotion and intellect, love and hatred, conformity and rejection, life and death. The characters of her novels are basically tragic, for even as they accept their destiny, they refuse to surrender: "Come now, we must not fret. If it must be so, we must learn to accept." (*Cry, the Peacock*, 54) A strong sense of individuality and their hypersensitive nature make them alienated and solitary. They suffer from a spiritual dilemma. The novelist portrays this by quoting a few lines from Cavafy:

> To certain people there comes a day when they must say the great Yes or the great No. He who has the Yes ready within him reveals himself at once, and saying it he crosses over to the path of honour and his own conviction. He who refuses does not repent should he be asked again, he would say No again! And yet that No—the right No—crushes him for the rest of his life. (*Where Shall We Go This Summer?*, 37)

It is the "great No" which these characters say to the society. They spend a secluded and withdrawn life, immersed in their own selves. Apart from their temperamental aloofness, the outside forces, such as the city, nature and family play major roles in making them morbid and tragic. The sordid and hollow life of the metropolis, the city's indifference and apathy to human emotions and feelings lead to a regressive tendency in the characters. Dissatisfied with their present, they turn back to the sweet days of the childhood. For some of the protagonists such as Maya, Sita, Monisha and Amla, the childhood is really beautiful but there are other characters who create an illusory world of childhood happiness like Nanda Kaul and try to get solace out of it. The impact of nature on the characters through her several agents such as moon, stars, seasons, flowers, and trees is also remarkable which make the protagonists conscious of the reality around them.

The physical, moral and spiritual misery of urban life results in alienation, loneliness and loss of human values and the protagonists fall victims to them. It eventually results in the attitude of defeat and disillusionment leading to preoccupation with the idea of death and dying.

Desai perhaps agrees with Dostoevski that "reason is inadequate." In *Notes from the Underground*, Dostoevski says: "Where did all the sages get the idea that a man's desire must be normal and virtuous? . . . What a man needs is simply and solely independent volition whatever that independently may cost and wherever it may lead." He further says: "What does reason know? Reason knows only what it has succeeded in finding out . . . but man's nature acts as one whole." (34) The men in Desal's novels, Raman, Gautama, Nirode and Jiban are "all reason" and the women, Maya, Sita, Monisha and Nanda are "all emotion." They represent respectively the prose and passion of life. Desai has attempted to strike a balance between intellect and emotion which can solve the existential problems of the protagonists.

Gautama takes the death of Toto as "missing the games you played with him" and ultimately the "empty time" calling for a "replacement." But for Maya the death of the dog is a prelude to another great disaster: "it was not my pet's death alone that I mourned today, but another sorrow, unremembered, perhaps as yet not even experienced and filled me with despair." (*Cry, the Peacock*, 8)

Besides the albino's prophecy and the death of Toto, the sordid life in the metropolis which she lives amidst Gautama's family members enhances her sorrow and deepens her sense of loneliness. In Gautama's family nobody speaks of love and affection. They only talk of discussions in the parliament, of corruption and bribery and of the newspaper editors accused of libel. Sometimes they play the game of cards "so swiftly, so nervously, so intently" that it seems as if they are trying to release the "mounting pressure by conversing and would begin to talk again of political scandal and intellectual dissent." (47) Gautama's mother would remark passing by Maya: "it was wise of Gautama to have married you." (47) She says this in a tone that is at once "soft and broken with harshness" so that Maya cannot say whether she said this out of affection or had some motives far removed from her feelings. She never cares for Maya except enquiring about the cheques which she needs to run her creche: "When will your father send me another cheque, Maya? Tell him I need it urgently—the nurses in the creche have not been paid this month." (47-48) This leads Maya to think that for her mother-in-law, she is not among the human beings whose comfort and health she felt responsible for, but one of the outsiders who "could be used for this purpose and were therefore necessary, though not necessarily loved." (48)

Maya also longs for the love and affection of her husband, to "touch" him, "feel his flesh and hair" and then to tighten her hold on him. She longs not for Gautama's love alone but of the entire "pulsating world" around him, from the silent stars to the fluttering owl "all that suggested life and the great entrancing world to me who was doomed not to live." (102) Gautama considers this too much attachment. He thinks Maya's father responsible for making her spoilt by fulfilling her every demand and showering too much love and affection on her. He thinks that Maya is tormented for taking delusion as happiness: "Yes, and all you ever knew was happiness was a crime! A crime because it was a delusion. And here you are capable of seeing nothing but delusions, imagining them to be real. How prettily you stroll in your garden, dreaming of the fairies that sleep in the buds." (105)

The squalor and sordidness of the metropolis has so affected the life-style of its inhabitants that they have become inhuman and indifferent like Gautama and his family members and Maya falls a victim to their callousness and apathy. She develops a regressive attitude and becomes nostalgic. She loses the balance of her mind, has unnatural dreams and hallucinatory experiences. She hears vibrations of drum-beats and wonders: "This is insanity. But who, what is insane? I myself? or the world around me?" (145) The thought of death deepens with the revival of the memory of the astrologer. She dreams more and more about him as the final and decisive year approaches. The call of the peacocks in the jungle makes her restless. Maya develops a love for a life-in-death which would be a release from her death-in-life existence. She wants to lose herself in eternal sleep, but she is unable to sleep and cries out in agony: "I am dying, and I am in love with living. I am in love and I am dying. God, let me sleep, forget, rest. But no, I will never sleep again. There is no rest any more—only death and waiting." (98)

The peacocks cry for their lovers. They are aware of death in living. Their mortal cry of agony is for their lovers and for death. Listening to the death-call of the peacocks Maya is taken back to her childhood through memory. Now she understands their call. She knows she can never again sleep in peace because she is "caught in the net of the inescapable." There is no possibility of release for her. She is perturbed by the thought of death but does not know who is to die. She mutters in her sleep, "But to perish? Who? Tell me who." Maya knows it is certain that death is to devour one of them, either Gautama or her: "who knows which one is to perish? Perish one must. The desert is waiting, the rats and the lizards. They will claim the flesh, the winds will carry the bones away." (127-28) The image of the lizard as an agent of death appears recurrently throughout the novel. Maya feels panic-stricken thinking about an imaginary death. She wonders whether it would be by fire or flood, whether there would be bloodshed or screams: "Will it be fire? Will it be flood? Will the lizards rise out of the desert to come up on us—either upon him or upon myself—with lashing tails and sliding tongues, to crush us beneath their bellies? Will there be blood? Will there be screams?" (179)

Maya gets confused thinking about the approaching death. Her thought process becomes chaotic, disordered. Thoughts and incidents get jumbled up and past, present, future get intermingled. She goes upstairs and from the roof-top looks at her garden which is in the process of decay: "The lawn is dying in irregular patches, yellow here, tawny there, green around the water-tap." (180)

The dust storm is followed by silence. Maya feels agitated and also humiliated by the thought of being neglected by Gautama. As both of them walk on the roof, Maya hears the omnious hooting of the owl. Gautama keeps silent and detaches himself completely into his "exclusive mind." At the parapet's edge, Maya makes him pause and his words are "lost" to her. She pushes him off the terrace and Gautama dies. Maya's obsession with death from the very beginning thus culminates in her hysteric act of killing Gautama. Maya finally avenges the death of Toto with the strange hope of escaping from the experience of dying in life.

Monisha's mean existence leads her to think that death is the only alternative to her agonised living, to her "confused despair": "The family here, and their surroundings tell me such a life cannot be lived—a life dedicated to nothing—that this husk is a protection from death. Ah, yes, then it is a choice between death and mean existence, and that surely is not a difficult choice." (*Voices in the City*, 122)

Monisha undergoes physical, moral and spiritual miseries in her in-laws's house. Her in-laws talk about her impossible family, about her organs, the reasons she cannot have a child. She is accused of theft, of taking money out of her husband's pocket. She thinks it would be better for her to live in solitude "a little beyond and below everyone else in exile." Monisha reflects on the utter lack of conscience in the city of Calcutta: "Has this city a conscience at all, this Calcutta that holds its head between its knees and grins toothlessly up at me from beneath a bottom black with the dirt that it sits on." (116)

The people of Calcutta represented by Monisha's in-laws are as cruel and rapacious as the city where there is no ethics except greed for money and fattening of human bodies: "Here they dwell, in these houses of cut-throats, eye for eye rapacity, of money greed and money ruthlessness to bless those who fatten upon it, to bless them and not to forgive." (117)

There is torture outside and also inside the family. Jiban's mother sniffs when she hears Monisha singing to Kalayani di's baby in its cradle. Kalayani di thinks her "dangerous" and an "infidel" because she always remains silent; "they all distrust silence." Like the crowd in the city of Calcutta, Monisha finds Jiban's house crowded with people; family members, guests and relatives.

Monisha is offered a ticket for a music concert given by their South Indian neighbour to her senior aunts. Since no one has interest in music, the ticket is given to Monisha and the old poor relation on the roof-top is asked to escort her. The family members regard music as dangerous. Monisha thinks perhaps they are right. Music is very dangerous as it brings her "to the edge" and she is plunged down into something "too intense to be borne."

The music players at the concert play different instruments and about everything. It seems to Monisha that there is nothing left unsaid: "There seems nothing left to say—not for human beings, city beings, body beings such as these, such as myself." (125)

Monisha gets confused. Life seems to her "only a conundrum" which is to "brood over forever with" passion and pain and never to arrive at a solution.

Monisha receives a letter from her younger sister Amla informing her about Amla's coming to Calcutta. While thinking about Amla, who has a career and talents, she feels Amla growing larger and larger than herself. She feels herself growing smaller everyday, "shrink and lose" more of her weight. She feels that her very existence is gradually becoming invisible and that it would reach the point of extinction one day: "I grow smaller everyday, shrink and lose more and more of my weight, my appurtenances, the symbols of my existence that used to establish me in the eyes of this world. I am already too small to be regarded much by anyone. I will be invisible yet." (139)

Monisha alone in the family remains untouched by the world outside. She considers her life to be a waste; a life that is locked in a steel container. Like Maya, she has not given birth to a child. She has also not attended death. She runs through the door of the room inside its "barred enclosure." A desire to be extinct envelops her. She wants to experience "feelings" and "desire" through fire; "to her astonishment the very first match struck fire" and the colour of the flame is golden and straight as a "promise kept." Her kerosene-soaked saree and blouse responds to the flame "with a leap of recognition; two elements had met, and in their embrace she was caught." (242) Monisha dies a cloistered death like her own cloistered life, "no ashes of that fire drifted over the city, no wind carried the smoke to inform others of the cloistered tragedy." (242-43)

While Monisha finds escape from her mean existence by accepting death, Nirode remains a defeatist all through his life. He is frustrated, depressed and highly independent minded, who thinks it is impossible on his part to work under any men. He changes from one profession to another and does not find satisfaction in any job. After his repeated failures, he becomes obsessed with the idea of failure: "I want to move from failure to failure, step by step to rock bottom." (40)

Because of his deep sense of failure and frustration, he wants to see beyond happiness and suffering: "Happiness, suffering—I want to be done with them, disregard them, see beyond them to the very end." (40)

Nirode feels the sense of defeat and failure run in his blood. It is congenital, "I was born with my heart emptied out," says Nirode in utter disappointment. He is a shadowy cipher whose life consists of "one dejection following another." He is full of contempt and loathing for the world "that could offer him no crusade, no pilgrimage." He is also full of loathing for himself for not having "the true, unwavering spirit of either within him." His own existence is hollowed out by an intrinisic knowledge that there is nothing to wait for but still there is no end to his waiting.

Monisha, Nirode and Amla have a sort of "terrible destructiveness" in them. It forms an integral part of their very personalities. They are basically pessimistic in their approach and attitude to life. Jit Nair reveals this trait in his conversation with Amla: "I don't understand it—this terrible destructiveness in all of you. You seem to worship it, shelter it inside yourself as though it were essential to you. Nothing will persuade you to forego it—not you, not your brother, nor that strange sister of yours." (175) Amla suspects that Jit finds them to be masochists. Jit observes that they have a "dreadful attractiveness" in their dark ways of thinking: "You destroy—you destroy yourselves and you destroy that part of others that gets so fatally involved in you. There is this—this dreadful attractiveness in your dark ways of thinking and feeling through life towards death." (175)

Jit finds Amla, Nirode and Monisha drive themselves deliberately towards the "dead end" where they think they will find "some divine solution." But they do not know that in death there is no solution as Jit has discovered in his own life: "but there is none, not in a life time all of us discover that and we force ourselves to turn and take another road." (176)

Monisha's death, Amla believes, has pointed the way for her and "would never allow her to lose herself." She is now prepared to accept the challenges of life, to go through life with her feet "primly shod," because Monisha has shown her a glimpse of what lies on the other side of the "stark, uncompromising margin." (248)

Nirode has been led into a greater realization of life by Monisha's death. He wants to reassure Amla and aunt that Monisha died from an "excess of caring" in a fire of care and conscience and that "they too must accept, with a like intensity." They should try to seize "each moment, each person, each fragment of the world, and reverence it with that acute care that had driven Monisha to her splendid death." (248)

The characters in *Bye-Bye, Blackbird* experience a different type of defeat and disillusionment. Sarah becomes a cultural exile in her own land by marrying a foreigner. She tries her best to keep up her identity despite her Indian husband but is defeated. She finally decides to go to India with her husband Adit. Adit betrays his self by adopting the citizenship of a foreign country and marrying a foreigner but he too is finally defeated in his adventure. At last he decides to return to his own country. Dev, for whom England was only "a cold wasteland of brick and tiles" gets "trapped" by the enchanting beauty of the English countryside.

When Adit informs Sarah about his desire to go back to India, Sarah also agrees to go with him. Adit feels nostalgic for his motherland. He feels he has been pretending all the time. Their lives in England have been so unreal: "All our records and lamb curries and sing-songs, it's so unreal. It has no reality at all, we just pretend all the time." (204)

When the flat is almost empty after all that was to be sold was sold and as they are preparing themselves to go to India, Sarah feels that Adit is going to "transport" her to a land where she would "regain warmth and personality." In that new land if she was to come to life again, that would be a different, and perhaps a better life. She must say good-bye to her English self: "It was her English self that was receding and fading and dying, she knew, it was her English self to which she must say good-bye." (221)

At the departure of Adit and Sarah on their journey to India, Dev murmurs to himself as a kind of "parting salute to them" and also as a "prayer" for himself:

> Make my bed and light the light,
> I will arrive late to night,
> Blackbird, bye-bye. (230)

Dev's prayer at the end is ironical. It is a farewell to the blackbird, the Indian immigrant, Adit, to his own nest. Like the indelible blackness of the blackbird, Adit and Dev cannot shed their Indianness despite staying in a foreign country. Adit accepts this reality of his Indianness and decides that his "son will be born in India." Sarah's loss of identity and the alienness among her own people in her own country leads her to the conclusion that going back to India with her husband would be the best solution to her problem of personal identity. Though Dev stays back in England for higher studies but in his "parting salute" to Adit and Sarah which is also a prayer for himself, there is a suggestion of acceptance of his real self: that Dev—the blackbird—will also feel obliged to return to its permanent nest in future.

Sita's decision to go to the island of Manori is both an escape and a return. It is an escape from the "destructive forces in the urban milieu." (N.R. Shastri, 87) It is also a return to the magic island for realizing the fantasy of "keeping the child unborn." A woman in her forties, a mother of four children, greying and aging does not want to give birth to her fifth child, because she is afraid of the violence that goes with the process of creation. The "madness" in the city, the violence and destructive attitude of its people, her husband's indifference and the callousness of the children drive her to think that it is better to escape into the primitive island of her father in Manori. The children fight among each other. Menaka has developed a destructive attitude which is revealed as she crushes the buds that had appeared in the plant which Sita had grown with much care. She destroys the painting which she herself had drawn. Raman and his family members do not have any finer sensibility. Only food, sex and money matter to them. Their "sub-human placidity" threatens Sita's very existence.

Sita's disillusionment is reflected in her behaviour and her decision.

Coming back to the island, Sita finds it adversely affected by the passage of time and changes in outlook. It is no more the island of her memory and dreams. The island cannot provide her "unity of being." (Sastri, 99) Sita realizes that life has no periods, no stretches. It simply "swirled around, muddling, confusing, leading nowhere." (*Where Shall We Go This Summer?*, 154-55) Looking back, she finds that she had spent twenty years of her life "connecting," eventually leading herself to a state of acute frustration. She comes to the realization that escaping to the island was a sheer illusion, like "an actress in a theatrical performance." She decides to return to the reality, to a life of "retirement, off stage."

After such a realization, Sita hopes that the "great gap" between her and Raman, would be newly and securely bridged." (151) Her decision to return to her husband signifies her defeat and failure on the one level and on the other suggests that "the facing of the sordid realities of life and the pilgrimage to the island have graduated her into acquiring a mature sensibility." (Asnani, *Indian Literature*, 51)

The death-suicide syndrome of Desai's earlier novels changes into a "sober, balanced acceptance of life" (N.R. Shastri, 83) in *Where Shall We Go This Summer?* Sita narrates the episode of the Muslim woman and declares to Raman that this is the most illuminating moment of her life. She was a very young woman, "fatally anaemic" or "fatally tubercular," looking pale and very beautiful lying on the lap of an old man. He was looking down at her and caressing her face so tenderly that it led Sita to think, "one does not see such an expression on human faces." It was quite divine. They made her see her own life like "a shadow, absolutely flat, uncoloured." Sita says to Raman, "that was the only time I have ever seen that life has meaning." She does not know whether her married years that she had spent in the metropolis or the escape to the past, to the island, were real or illusory. She gets confused and shakes her head angrily at the confusion, at the muddle: "Neither sea nor sky were separate or contained—they rushed into each other in a rush of light and shade, impossible to disentangle." (153) She gets herself prepared to go back to Bombay as she realizes that "life must be continued and all its business." (138)

Nanda Kaul had practised an hour of stillness everyday for years:

> She had practised this stillness, this composure for years, for an hour every afternoon: it was an art, not easily acquired. . . . She remembered how she had tried to shut out sound by shutting out light, how she had spent the sleepless hour making out the direction from which a shout came, or a burst of giggles. All was subdued, but nothing was over still. (*Fire on the Mountain*, 23)

In the Vice-Chancellor's house "doors were never shut and feet flew, or tramped without ceasing." (23) From all sides sounds entered her room. Throughout her life she had yielded to a pattern, submitted to the requirements of her husband's status. So coming to Carignano, Nanda Kaul wants nothing, no one around her. Whatever would come or happen would be an "unwelcome intrusion and distraction." She wants to achieve absolute solitude, to merge with the lonely pine tree and to be one with it.

The postman's letter informing her about her great grand-daughter's arrival comes as the first intrusion. The phone call of Ila Das also reminds her of her past busy life. She deliberately avoids Raka and postpones Ila's visit to Carignano. But to her surprise she finds that Raka is totally absorbed in her own world without being bothered about her great grandmother. Raka ignores Nanda with a "total rejection, so natural, instinctive and effortless." (47) If Nanda Kaul has arrived at this condition of absolute loneliness after many rejections and sacrifices, Raka is born to it. Nanda Kaul discovers Raka totally different from other children. She is not worried about anything except being left alone in the bare and empty hills of Kasauli. Nanda Kaul also discovers that Raka is very much like her. She tries to attract her attention by creating a world of fantasy about her own childhood, because Raka's indifference becomes a challenge to her.

Ila Das's arrival is the second shock to Nanda Kaul's illusory world as it again reminds her of the stark realities which cannot be evaded by coming over to Kasauli. The visit of Ila Das reminds Nanda of her past, her school days. She opens the "unwilling gate" and invites Ila to enter:

> Here she came, Ila Das, still little Ila Das, with what remained of the pig tail wound on top of her head like a tea-cosy, an egg-cosy, yellowed rather than whitened by age, and Nanda Kaul looked down from her height having invited her to tea, having failed to put her away out of sight and mind. Here she was, that last little broken bit of a crazy life, fluttering up over the gravel like a bit of crumpled paper. (112)

With the rape and murder of Ila Das, the illusory world of Nanda gets shattered to pieces and the fire that Raka sets suggests its ultimate consumption. The "fire" may be taken as the fire of love that Raka generates in the heart of Nanda Kaul. It may also be taken as the symbol of pyre—the funeral fire, and ultimate consumption of the fictive world of Nanda Kaul.

The question of acceptance comes in relation to Time in Desai's

Clear Light of Day which reflects the ideas of Marcel Proust's *Remembrance of Things Past* and T.S. Eliot's *Four Quartets*. The central characters of this novel, Tara and Bim, are not prepared to accept the passage of time. Tara is not prepared to accept the present, being deeply engrossed in her past and for Bim, time has ravaged her old relationships and created a changed pattern of relationship in the family. Gradually Tara accepts the dictates of time. But Bim takes some time to realize this. Towards the end of the novel, Desai refers to music and song. The difference of voice between Mulk and his Guru leaves a deep impression on Bim. Mulk's child-like "sweet and clear" voice is counterpoised against the oldman's "sharp" and "a little cracked" voice mingled with "bitterness," "sadness," "passion" and frustration. The old man sang like a man "who had come, at the end of his journey, within sighting distance of death so that he already stood in its looming presence and measured the earth and his life on it by that great shadow." (192) In spite of the difference in their voices, there is a similarity between them: they belong to the same school and have the same style of singing. Listening to the song, Bim is suddenly reminded of Eliot's *Four Quartets:* "Time the destroyer is time the preserver." It leads her to reflect on the interpenetration of time past and time present:

> With her inner eye she saw how her own house and its particular history linked and contained her as well as her whole family with all their separate histories and experiences not binding them within some dead and airless cell but giving them the soil in which to send down their roots, and food to make them grow and spread, reach out to new experiences and new lives, but always drawing from the same soil, the same secret darkness. (182)

She also realizes that in that soil her "deepest self lived" and that the soil contains all time "past and future." It is "dark with time, rich with time." (182)

Desai's message "to connect" in order to exist also reverberates in her novel *In Custody*. The protagonist Deven is resigned to the life of a lecturer in an obscure college in the dusty, shapeless town of Mirpore. Throughout his childhood and youth he has learned to "lie low and invisible." Deven goes to Delhi to interview the great living poet Nur and finds that his dream has turned to a disaster. The Nur of his dream is in reality a weak, gasping old man whose creative days are long since over. But the novel ends with a note of optimism when Deven has a vision of Nur's bier heaped with "bright blaring flowers," with his women weeping and wailing all around. This vision of death is also a vision of life—

an assertion of the immortality of the artist. The relation between the two is indestructible. Deven would become the custodian of "Nur's very soul and spirit." (204) The occurrence of positive images like the "pampass grass" waving and rustling with "life, rippling sound" suggests hope and life. The day would be bright though it would be accompanied by calamities. Life will continue in spite of them.

The theme of displacement in *Bye-Bye, Blackbird* is repeated in *Baumgartner's Bombay* with a little variation, where there is a possibility of redemption for Adit and Sarah, for Baumgartner, there is none. There is no land which he can call his own. Germany he has left behind and there is no possibility of going back there and India, he has made his own but the land is not prepared to accept him. He is too uncertain of his future as if uncertainty has become a part of his life. He is brutally murdered by the boy whom he had given shelter. Thus he dies in innocence, as if innocence has become an element with him.

Bewilderment, rejection and solitude torment Baumgartner all through his life. He wonders at his ability to survive amidst such an abject state of helplessness. Inside the internment camp with the fellow prisoners he felt lonely as if he had no friend. That inherent sense of loneliness haunted him when he was alone as well as when he was in company: "It was not any of them regarded him as a friend: it was that with them he could pretend he was solitary. Outside, he would be that—a man without a family or a country." (133)

Germany has betrayed him by separating him from his mother. In India he is deceived, arrested, put in prison, humiliated, being considered a "firanghi" and at last stabbed to death. The struggle for existence in which Baumgartner is engaged is the very essence of human predicament. Like him everyone is inevitably engaged in one or the other kind of war: "War within was within war everyone engaged in a separate war, and each was opposed to another war. If they could be kept separate, chaos would be averted." (173)

Lotte is yet another victim of the struggle for existence, she has failed in her attempts to be an Indian bride. Married to Kanti Sethia, rejected by his family, she stays in a different house which Kanti seldom visits. He comes to Lotte when he is in need of a change. Lotte, though neglected and rejected, yet observes all the Hindu rituals and tries her best to be like a Hindu bride. But after Kanti's death his son comes and drives her out of the house which Kanti had purchased for her. Thus Lotte spends a life of utter loneliness without a family, a country and an identity of her own. She confesses: "Mostly I am alone. All, all alone." (203)

Being cut off from the mainstream, Baumgartner and Lotte spend the lives of exiles. For them life has been reduced to nothingness. There is no hope for future. But they discover a different pleasure in this nothingness: "Nothing, this was what life dwindled down to, but Baumgartner found he enjoyed that nothing more than he had enjoyed anything." (211)

Behind the curtain that divides Baumgartner's private territory from the mainstream, he has learnt to live, a different kind of life, without any interruption from the crowd at the other side of the hectic and chaotic life beyond the curtain:

> He felt his life a blur, turn grey a curtain wrapping him in its dusty felt. If he became aware, from time to time, that the world beyond the curtain was growing steadily more crowded, more clamorous and the lives of others more hectic, more chaotic, then he felt only relief that he had never been part of the mainstream. Always somehow he had escaped the mainstream. (211)

Through a number of evocative images, Desai portrays the basic human problems and the anguish of the lonely soul. In spite of all apparent relationships, man is alone. No human relationship can relieve him of his existential problems. To quote Anita Desai's own words: "I think all human relationships are incomplete. I have never worked this out. Basically everyone is solitary. I think involvement in human relationship in this world invariably leads to disaster." ("Interview," *Stairs to the Attic,* 12) The loss of moral and spiritual moorings leads the characters to an intense awareness of futility. Though they are defeated in the battle of life, they do not surrender their individuality. On the other hand, they accept stoically the challenges of life.

Anita Desai's vision of life is one of ambivalence, born out of an awareness of paradoxes at various levels. Her fictional world is a world of defeat and disillusionment on the one hand and on the other of compromises and reconciliations. Memory and dream, joy and suffering, disillusionment and hallucination, individual and community are the central preoccupations around which revolves Desai's perception of the paradoxes. In the process of realizing these paradoxes Desai's characters undergo a process of suffering and purgation. The assertion of the existential reality of the individual against the forces of chaos and disintegration creates a profound sense of tragic tension. The experience of defeat and disillusionment in Anita Desai's fiction not only leads to agony and suffering but also to an acquiescence of life. The protagonists of Anita Desai confront with courage the sordid realities of life that threaten to submerge the individual self in the welter of cosmopolitanism and social obligations. Though they often fail in their mission, their confrontation assumes a tragic dimension in terms of their anguish and profound introspection. They are tormented souls who, in their death-in-life, aspire towards life-in-death. It is in this sense that Desai's fictional world reflects a tragic sense of life.

Bibliography

1. Primary Sources

A. Novels

Cry, the Peacock. London: Peter Owen, 1963. New Delhi: Orient, 1990.
Tipatul Panulai Rumani. Colectia Meridiane, 1966.
Voices in the City. London: Peter Owen, 1965. New Delhi: Orient, 1982.
Bye-Bye, Blackbird. Delhi: Hind Pocket Books, 1971. New Delhi: Orient, 1985.
Where Shall We Go This Summer? Delhi: Vikas, 1975. New Delhi: Orient, 1991.
Fire on the Mountain. London: William Heinemann, 1977.
Clear Light of Day. London: William Heinemann, 1980.
In Custody. USA: Harper and Row, 1984. London: Heinemann, 1988.
Baumgartner's Bombay. Penguin Books, 1989.

B. Short Stories

Games at Twilight. London: William Heinemann, 1978. Includes "Pinapple Cake," "Studies in the Park," "The Farewell Party," "Scholar and Gipsy," and "Games at Twilight."
Village by the Sea: A Long Story. 1982.

C. For Children

The Peacock Garden. Bombay: Indian Book House, 1974.
Cat on a Houseboat. Bombay: Orient Longman, 1976.
"Circus Cat, Alley Cat," *Thought,* 1957.
"How Gentle is the Mist," *The Illustrated Weekly of India*, 1958.
"Grand Mother," *Miscellany,* Calcutta: Writers' workshop, 1960.
"An Examination," *Miscellany,* 1960.
"To Seal a Picture," *Miscellany*, 1960.
"Tea with the Maharani," *Envoy,* 1959.
"Ghost House," *Quest,* 1961.

"Mr. Bose's Private Bliss," *Envoy,* 1959.
"Private Tution by Mr. Bose," *Indian Literature,* 1970.
"Descent from the Rooftop," *The Illustrated Weekly of India*, 1970.
"Surface Textures," *Femina,* 1974
"The Accompanist," *Quest,* 1975.

D. Articles

"Calcutta Kaleidoscope," *The Illustrated Weekly of India,* 1958.
"Women Writers," *Quest*, 65, April-June, 1970, 39-43.
"Pilgrimage," *The Illustrated Weekly of India,* 1966.
"Gangtok," *Envoy,* 1959.
"The Indian Writer's Problems," *Language Forum,* VIII, 1-4, April 1981-March 1982, 223-25.
"The Timid Movement of a Wing," *The Indian Literary Review,* August 1978.
"Jhabvala, A Sure Winner," *The Illustrated Weekly of India,* 7 March 1976, 1-6.
Book Review of *Hymns in Darkness* by Nissim Ezekiel, *The IPEN,* March-April 1977, 3-4.
"Contemporary English Literature in India," *Littcrit*, 8, Jan. 1982, 65-68.
"Literary Lapses," *Book Review*, VII, 1, July/Aug. 1982, 8-10.
"Flight of Forms," *Indian International Centre Quarterly,* 10:4, 1983, 409-24.
"The Novelist who writes for herself," *The Journal of Indian Writing in English,* July 1977.
"Book I Enjoyed Writing Most," *Contemporary Indian Literature,* 13:4, Oct-Dec. 1973, 23-24.
"Inner Sphere," Review of *The Circle of Reason, India Today,* March 15, 1986, 149.
"A Kulu Christmas," *Envoy,* 1959.
"Within and Without Tradition," *ACLALS News Letter,* 5, April 1979, 5-21.
"Memoirs of a Mendicant Professor, A Review," *Quest,* 66, July-Sept. 1970.

F. Interviews

Dalmia, Yasodhara. "An Interview with Anita Desai," *The Times of India,* 29 April 1979.
Jain, Jasbir. "Anita Desai Interviewed," *Rajasthan University Studies in English*, XII, 1979, 61-69.

Ram, Atma. "An Interview with Anita Desai," *World Literature Written in English*, 16, 1, Nov. 1977, 95-104.
"Replies to the Questionnaire," *Kakatiya Journal of English Studies*, III, 1, 1978, 1-6.
"Where are the Errors," Interview by HK, *The Hindustan Times*, 20 November 1983, 1-5.

II. Secondary Sources

Acharya, Shanta. "Problems of the Self in the Novels of Anita Desai," *Language Forum*, 7, 1-4, April 1981-March 1982, 236-54.
Alcock, Peter. "Rope, Serpent, Fire—The Recent Fiction of Anita Desai," *Journal of Indian Writing in English*, IX, 1, Jan. 1981, 15-34.
Alladi, Uma. "To Accept or Reject: The Woman as Wife," *The Literary Criterion*, XX, 4, 1985, 79-90.
Allen, Walter. *The English Novel*. Pelican Books, 1958.
Amin, Amina. "Imagery as Mode of Apprehension in Anita Desai's Novels," *Littcrit*, 10, 1, 1984, 36-44.
Asnani, Shyam M. "Anita Desai's Fiction: A New Dimension," *Indian Literature*, 24, 2, Mar.-Apr. 1981, 47-54.
______. "Themes of Withdrawal and Loneliness in Anita Desai's *Fire on the Mountain*," *Journal of Indian Writing in English*, IX, 1, Jan. 1981, 81-92.
______. "Anita Desai—The Novelist with Unique Personal Vision," *Contemporary Indian Thought*, 14, 1, Jan-March 1974, 6, 9, 16-21.
Bande, Usha. *The Novels of Anita Desai*. New Delhi: Prestige, 1988.
Banerjee, Purabi. "Bookworm's Progress," *Statesman*, 16 April 1983.
Belliappa, Meena. *Anita Desai: A Study of Her Fiction*. Calcutta: Writers' Workshop, 1971.
Bhatnagar, K.C. *Realism in Major Indo-English Fiction*. Bareilly: Prakash, 1980.
Brooks, Cleanth. "The Language of Paradox," *Literary Criticism*. Calcutta: Oxford Univ. Press.
Brook, M.W. and W.J. Hardy. "Irony as a Principle of Structure," *Twentieth Century Criticism*. Delhi: Light and Life Publishers.
Castillege, Irene Claremont de. *Knowing Woman—A Feminine Psychology*, 1973; New York: Harper and Colophon, 1974.
Conrad, Joseph. Preface to *The Nigger of the Narcissus*, 1914.
Daffry, Nayana. "Review of *Cry, the Peacock*," *Quest*, Autumn Review, 10, 1, 1983, Winter 50.
Dhawan, R.K. *Explorations in Modern Indo-English Fiction*. Delhi:

Bahri, 1982.

______. *Commonwealth Fiction*. New Delhi: Classical, 1987.

______. *The Fiction of Anita Desai*. New Delhi: Prestige, 1988.

______, et al. *Recent Commonwealth Literature*. New Delhi: Prestige, 1989.

Dostoevski, Fudor. *Notes from the Underground*. Penguin.

Dua, M.R. "Anita Desai," *Femina*, 4 Jan. 1974, 25.

Dudt, Charmazel. "Past and Present: A Journey to Confrontation," *Journal of Indian Writing in English*, IX, 1, 1981, 67-73. A Study of *Where Shall We Go This Summer?*

Forster, E.M. *Aspects of the Novel*. Penguin International, 1962.

______. *Howards End*. Penguin International, 1976.

Gabriel, A. "Anita Desai's *Fire on the Mountain*—A Review," *Times Literary Supplement*, 17 June 1977, 721.

Ganguli, Chandra. "*Fire on the Mountain*," *Commonwealth Quarterly*, 6, 2, Dec. 1981, 40-44.

Gokak, V.K. "The Concept of Indianness with Reference to Indian Writing in English," *Indian Writing in English*, ed. Ramesh Mohan. Madras: Orient Longman, 1978, 21-25.

Goyal, B.S. "The World of Women Novelists," *The Hindustan Times Weekly*, 4, 12, Jan. 69, 64-69.

Gupta, G.S. Balarama. *Studies in Indian Fiction in English*. Gulbarga: JIWE.

Hashim, A. "A Review of *Clear Light of Day*," *International Fiction*, 1963, 99-101.

Heinemann, F.H. *Existentialism and the Modern Predicament*. London: Adam and Charles Black, 1959.

Iyengar, K.R. Srinivasa. *Indian Writing in English*. New Delhi : Sterling, 1964.

______. "A Note on Anita Desai's Novels," *BP*, 4, XII, 1976, 464-69.

Jain, Jasbir. *Stairs to the Attic: The Novels of Anita Desai*. Jaipur: Printwell, 1987.

______. "Anita Desai," *Indian English Novelists*, ed. Madhusudan Prasad. New Delhi: Sterling, 23-50.

______. "Use of Fantasy in the Novels of Anita Desai," *Explorations in Modern Indo-English Fiction*, ed. R.K. Dhawan. Bahri, 1982.

Jain, Madhu. "Anita Desai: Pretty Flower in a Wasteland." *New Delhi*, 24 Nov. 1980, 81-82.

Jamkhandi, Sudhakar Ratnakar. "Artistic Effects of the Shifts in the Point of View in Anita Desai's *Cry, the Peacock*," *Journal of Indian Writing in English*, IX, 1, Jan. 1981, 35-46.

Jung, C.G. *Practices of Psychotherapy. Collected Works*, 16, 20, trans.

R.F.S. Hull. Bollingen Series, 1954, Princeton University Press, 1970.

Kanwar, Asha. *Virginia Woolf and Anita Desai: A Comparative Study.* New Delhi: Prestige, 1989.

Kettle, Arnold. *An Introduction to the English Novel.* New Delhi: BI.

King, Francis. "Misfortune of a Fau," *Spectator*, 20, Oct. 1984, 35-36.

Kohli, Suresh. "Indian Women Novelists in English," *Times Weekly,* Nov. 1970.

Krishna, Francine E. "A Lulled Life: Review of *Where Shall We Go This Summer?*" *Quest*, 99, Jan-Feb. 1976.

______. "Anita Desai: *Fire on the Mountain*," *Indian Literature*, 25, 5, Sep.-Oct. 1982, 58-89.

Kumar, Shiv K. "The Fiction of Anita Desai: Another View," *The Humanist Review*, III, 2, 43-46.

Lal, P. "Review of *Voices in the City*," *Littcrit*, 2, 2, Dec. 1970, 51-53.

Lodge, David. *Language of Fiction.* London: Routledge and Paul.

Lubbock, Percy. *The Craft of Fiction*. New Delhi: BI, 1954. Rep. 1979.

Lucas, F.L. *Style*. London: Cassell, 1964.

Maini, Darshan Singh. "*Cry, the Peacock* as a Poetic Novel," *English Literature of the Past Fifty Years, 1917-67*, ed. C.D. Narasimhaiah. Mysore University, 1970, 225-34.

______. "The Achievement of Desai," *Indo-English Literature*, ed. K.K. Sharma. Ghaziabad: Vimal, 1977, 222.

Maini, Irma. "Anita Desai and the Feminine Sensibility," *Commonwealth Quarterly*, 9:28, 1984, 1-12.

______. "Achievements of Anita Desai." *Indo-English Literature*, ed. K.K. Sharma. Ghaziabad: Vimal, 1977, 215-30.

Mark, Schorer. "Technique as Discovery," *Twentieth Century Criticism*, ed. William J. Hardy and Max West Brook. New Delhi: Light and Life Publishers.

Masilamani. J.G. "Feminism in Anita Desai," *Kakatiya Journal of English Studies*, III, 1, 1978, 25-31.

Melwani, Murli Das. "Short Stories of Anita Desai," *Economic Times*, 29 April 1979, 4-6.

______. *Themes in Indo-Anglian Literature*. Bareilly: Prakash.

Mehta, P.P. *Indo-Anglian Fiction—An Assessment*. Bareilly: Prakash, 1988.

Mukherjee, Meenakshi. "The Theme of Displacement in Anita Desai and Kamala Markandaya," *World Literature Written in English*, 17, 1, April 1978, 225-32.

______. *The Twice Born Fiction*. New Delhi: Arnold Heinemann, 1971.

______. "Four Indo-Anglian Novels," *The Miscellany,* No. 39, June 1970,

27-33.

______. "A Review of *Bye-Bye Blackbird*," *Quest*, No. 7, March-April 1972, 96-98.

Muir, Edwin. *Structure of the Novel*. Indian edn. 1966.

Narasimhan, R. "Desai vs. Desani," *Indian Literature*, July-December 1973.

Narasimhaiah, C.D., ed. "*Voices in the City*," *Quest*, 48, Jan.-March 1966, 108-10.

Pandeya, Shiva M. *Studies in Modern Fiction*. New Delhi: Vikas, 1989.

______. "Sensibility under Stress," *Aspects of Indian English Fiction*. Delhi: Ashajanak, 1976.

Paul, S.K. *Cry, the Peacock: A Critical Study*. New Delhi: Harman, 1991.

Parasuram, Laxmi. "Mountain, New Dimension of Feminine Self Perception," *Literary Criterion*, XVI, 3, 1981, 58-64.

Prasad, Harimohan. "Sound or Sense: A Study of Anita Desai's *Bye-Bye, Blackbird*," *Journal of Indian Writing in English*, 9, 1, 1981, 58-66.

Prasad, Madhusudan. "*Where Shall We Go This Summer?* A Critical Study," *Rajasthan Journal of English Studies*, 13-14, 1981, 62-68.

______. "*Voices in the City*—A Critical Study," *Littcrit*, 7, 2, 1981, 46-58.

______. "*Fire on the Mountain*—An Assessment," *Journal of Literature and Aesthetics*, I, IV, 1981.

______. *Anita Desai: The Novelist*. Allahabad: New Horizon, 1986.

Ram, Atma. "Island on the Island: Anita Desai's *Where Shall We Go This Summer?*," *World Literature Written in English*, IV, 2, Nov. 1976, 381-83.

______. "Anita Desai: Exploration of Inner Sensibility," *Perspective*, July 1978, 54-55.

______. "Indians Slow to Recognize Talent in Their Midst," *Tribune*, 26 June 1977.

______. "Anita Desai," *National Herald*, 26 June 1980.

______. "A View of *Where Shall We Go This Summer?*," *Journal of Indian Writing in English*, IX, 1, Jan. 1981, 74-80.

______. "Shiv K. Kumar and Anita Desai: New Dimension to Indian English Fiction," *Triveni*, 52, 1984, 32-36.

______. "Anita Desai: A Bibliography," *The Journal of Indian Writing in English*, 9, 1, 1981, 93-98.

______. "Anita Desai's *Where Shall We Go This Summer?*: An Analysis," *Commonwealth Quarterly*, 10, 3, Mar. 1979.

Rao, B. Ramachandra. *The Novels of Anita Desai*. Delhi: Kalyani, 1977.

______. "Themes and Variations in the Novels and Short Stories of Anita Desai," *Journal of Literature and Aesthetics*, II, 2-3, 1982, 74-79.

Rao, A. Ramakrishna. "Anita Desai's Modernist's Novel," *The Literary Endeavour*, II, 1, 1981.

Rao, C.V. "Anita Desai," *The Tribune*, 2 April 1978.

Rao, Maithili. "Landscape of the Mind," *Eve's Weekly*, 6 Aug. 1983, 52-55.

Rao, Raja. *Kanthapura*. 1938.

Rao, Shyamala B. "Women Writers in Indo-Anglian Fiction," *Century*, 26 Jan. 1972, 25-34.

Rao, Vimala. "Anita Desai's *Where Shall We Go This Summer?*: An Analysis," *Commonwealth Quarterly*, 3, 9, Dec. 1978, 44-50.

Rabkin, Eric. *The Fantastic in Literature*. New Jersey: Princeton University, 1976.

Ramamurti, K.S. "The Indian Women Novelists Writing in English," *Littcrit*, 4, 1, June 1978, 33-41.

Reddy, G.A. *Indian Writing in English and Its Audience*. Bareilly: Prakash.

Reuben, Elizabeth. "Anita Desai's *Fire on the Mountain*," *World Literature Written in English*, 17, 1, April 1978.

Review of *Cry, the Peacock*, *Nagpur Times*, 15 December 1968.

Review of *Cry, the Peacock*, *The Times Literary Supplement*, no. 3, Friday, 22 Feb. 1963.

Roger, Iredale. "Anita Desai's *Cry, the Peacock*: The Father in the Unconscious," *Tenor*, 2, January 1979, 59-68.

Sengupta, Ranjana. "Sunlight through Chinks," *The Hindustan Times*, 26 Oct. 1980, 8-14.

Sharma, D.R. "Anita Desai," *The Tribune*, 2 Apr. 1978.

Sharma, R.S. *Anita Desai*. New Delhi: Arnold Heinemann, 1981.

______. "Movement and Stillness in Anita Desai's *Fire on the Mountain*," *Littcrit*, IV, 2, Dec. 1978, 1-6.

______. "Mother and the City—Archetypes in *Voices in the City*," *Journal of Literary Studies*, II, 2, Dec. 1979, 57-77.

______. "Anita Desai's *Where Shall We Go This Summer?*: An Analysis," *Commonwealth Quarterly*, III, 10, Mar. 1979.

______. "Alienation, Accommodation and the Locale in Anita Desai's *Bye-Bye, Blackbird*," *Literary Criterion*, 14, 4, 1979, 31-49.

Shastri, N.R. "*Where Shall We Go This Summer?* A Critical Study," *Osmania Journal of English Studies*, XVII, 1981, 83-103.

Sivaramakrishna, M. "From Alienation to Mythic Acceptance: The Ordeal of Consciousness in Anita Desai's Fiction," *Kakatiya Journal of English Studies* III, 1, 1978, 7-24.

Singh, R.S. "Aloneness Alone: Anita Desai and Arun Joshi," *Indian Novel in English*. New Delhi: Arnold-Heinemann, 1977.

Singh, R.K. *Indian Writing in English: Experiments with Expression*. New Delhi: Bahri.

Srivastava, N. "Some Indian Women Writers in English," *Indian Literature*, XVII, 4, 1975, 63-72.

Srivastava, Ramesh Kumar, ed. *Perspectives of Anita Desai*. Ghaziabad: Vimal, 1983.

______. *Six Indian Novelists*. Amritsar: GND Univ.

______. "Voices of Artists in the City," *Journal of Indian Writing in English*, IX, 1, Jan. 1981, 47-57.

Thomas, Van Lann. *Idioms of Drama*. Ithaca and London: Cornwell University Press, 1970.

Varady, Evelyne. "American and British Responses to Anita Desai's *Games at Twilight and Other Stories*," *Journal of Indian Writing in English*, 8, 1-2, Jan.-July 1980, 27-34.

Watt, Ian. *The Rise of the Novel*. London: Chatto and Windus, 1960.

Wayne C. Booth. *The Rhetoric of Fiction*. Chicago: The University of Chicago Press, 1961.

______. "Telling and Showing," *20th Century Criticism*, William J. Hardy and Max West Brook.

Weir, Ann Lowry. "Anita Desai's *Fire on the Mountain*," *World Literature Written in English*, VII, 2, Nov. 1978, 548-50.

______. "The Illusion of Maya, Feminine Consciousness in Anita Desai's *Cry, the Peacock*," *Journal of South Asian Literature*, XVI, 2, Summer 1981, 1-4.

Whitmont, Edward C. *The Symbolic Quest: Basic Concepts of Analytical Psychology*. New York: Harper and Colophon, 1969, rpt. 1973.

Williams, H.M. *Indo-Anglian Literature 1800-1970, A Survey*. Madras: Orient Longman, 1976.

Index